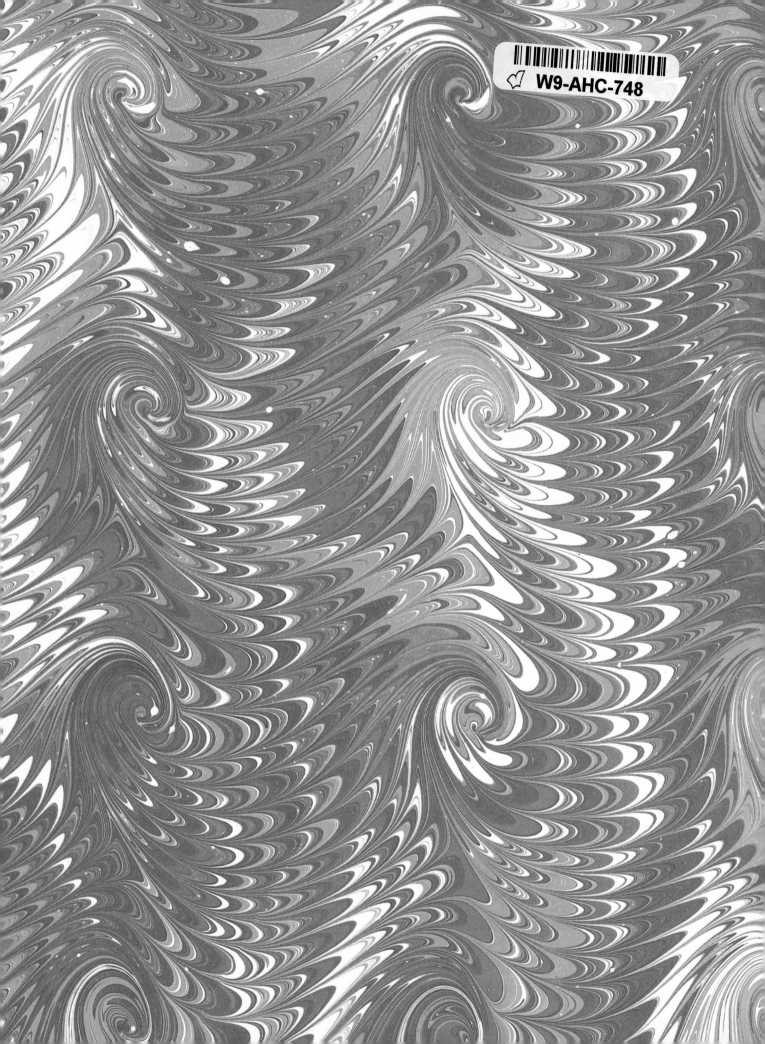

BATTERY TOYS

BATTERY TOYS
The Modern Automata

by Brian Moran

Schiffer Publishing Ltd

Box E, Exton, Pennsylvania 19341

Printed in the United States of America
ISBN: 0-88740-003-5
Published by Schiffer Publishing Ltd., Box E, Exton, Pennsylvania 19341

This book may be purchased from the publisher.
Please include $1.50 postage.
Try your bookstore first.

TABLE OF CONTENTS

ACKNOWLEDGMENTS

I would like to thank the following people, without whose help this project would have been much more difficult, if not impossible: Carol Buchman, Joan and Abe Cohen, Nancy and Bill Moran, Jean and Joe Placente of Gallery 802 Antiques, and Stephie and Paul Sadagursky of Happy Days.

I would like to extend a very special thank-you to Mr. F.H. Griffith, Mr. Dale Kelley, and my wife, Barbara.

INTRODUCTION

Pre-WWII German windup boat with battery operated lights.

Before World War I the majority of the tin mechanical toys imported to our country came from France and Germany. After the war, a new country entered the race. That country was Japan. The early Japanese toys were for the most part simple copies of existing European and American toys. Although they may have lacked something in originality, they had one big advantage over their competition. Because of cheap labor and low production costs, they were less expensive. Over the next decade or so, that one fact helped the Japanese toy makers take a large bite out of the world market.

During the years of the Second World War, since Japan and the rest of the world had more important things to do with their factories and metal was needed for the war effort, the tin toy all but disappeared.

After the war, the Japanese took up where they left off, and soon became the leading producer of toys and novelties for export to the United States. Using inexpensive scrap materials, such as tin beer and soda cans left by American soldiers, the Japanese produced an incredible variety of toys during the late 1940's and early 1950's. The combination of cheap labor and cheap materials made the Japanese very difficult to compete with. The great success of their toy industry was a very important factor in helping the Japanese economy back on its feet.

As conditions improved, so did the quality of the toys produced. After thirty years of being imitators, the toy makers of Japan became innovators. The innovation took the form of the battery driven motor as a source of power for the actions of the toy. This turned out to be the most important development in mechanical toy production since the keywind spring driven motor. This is not to say that no toys produced before this time used the dry cell as a power source. One American toy from the 1920's featured a Black dancing man who worked on a voice activated battery driven motor. A few cars, trucks and boats that ran on friction or wind-up motors had battery powered lights. But these toys were rare exceptions, and certainly did not have a major impact on the toy business as a whole. That changed in the 1950's and 1960's, when the Japanese promoted the battery toy from a sideshow novelty to a full-fledged star.

Suddenly, these battery toys were doing things that their predecessors, the wind-ups, could only dream about. Robots were walking around with a lighted screen on their chests that showed moving pictures of the moon, foxes were blowing soap bubbles and making rabbits disappear with the touch of a wand (and the help of an electro-magnet), parrots were flapping their wings and repeating every word you spoke, and men were blowing smoke from their ears, noses, mouths, stomachs, and derrieres.

The Japanese are no longer major producers of battery toys. They are too busy producing computers, cars, and cameras. Today the cheap labor is found in Hong Kong, Taiwan, and Korea. They are making today's playthings, but these recent toys don't have the beauty or ingenuity of their Japanese forerunners. They are simply poor copies of those wonderful originals. The only original toys being produced today come from mainland China. While they don't quite measure up to the Japanese toys, they are well made and interesting, and will undoubtedly someday be collectible.

The battery-operated toy reigned supreme for two decades, but progress marches on. The 70's brought the biggest change ever to hit the toy business. The computer chip made the battery toy seem primitive and obsolete. As sales of video games go up and up, the battery toy is slowly sinking into oblivion.

I grew up in the sixties and there was a special thrill in seeing a battery operated remote control Frankenstein standing menacingly under my Christmas tree. Today's kids get a square plastic box that gets stuck into their square plastic home video game so they can play Pac Man on TV. Maybe I'm getting old, but it just doesn't seem the same to me.

Top Row: *Assortment of recent Hong Kong and Taiwan toys.*
Bottom Row: *Tin spaceship and camel made in Red China.*

COLLECTING BATTERY OPERATED TOYS

I've been collecting and selling battery operated toys since the early 1970's, and while I don't pretend to know everything about them, I've learned enough to know that there are certain things that are very important and certain things that are not. Briefly, condition, rarity and desirability are important. Age and the toy's manufacturer are not. In post war Japanese toys, more than any other collectible toys, these priorities are often confused.

Of the three things that determine the value of a battery toy, first and most important is condition. In other areas of toy collecting, such as early cast iron or hand-painted tin, a toy with 50% of its original paint that is missing a part or two can still bring enormous amounts of money. I don't know of one major battery-toy collector who would ever consider buying an incomplete battery toy with only 50% of its original paint. Mint examples in the original boxes are naturally most desirable. Eliminate the box and you can cut an average of 25% off the value of the toy. If that same toy shows a fair amount of wear and tear, you can reduce its value by an additional 25%. Add some rust or missing parts and the value is reaching microscopic levels. So as a simple rule, try to buy battery toys in very good or better condition, preferably in the original box.

The second major factor in valuing a battery operated toy is its rarity, and the third is its desirability. While these two terms seem to be similar, there is a difference. A toy is rare because there are few examples of it available. A toy is desirable because a large number of collectors want to own it. Just because a toy is rare does not mean it is desirable. The Mickey Magician is not a particularly rare toy, yet it is one of the more desirable ones. A Bartender with rolling eyes is much harder to find but even harder to sell. It is simply not desirable. Combine a unique action and interesting subject matter with rarity and fine condition and you are making a wise choice. The toy you've picked should continue to increase in value in the years ahead.

Now for a few words on the relatively unimportant considerations in the Japanese toy collecting field. I've often had toys offered to me with "It's a Cragstan" added as a selling point. What some people don't seem to understand is that Cragston didn't manufacture toys,

they only imported and distributed them. Over the years they probably had many fine toys, and probably just as many that were of a much lower quality. Quite often, the same toy would have Cragstan's name on the box one year, and Linemar's name the following year, and maybe Rosko's the year after that. If you want to collect toys of a specific toy company, look for Lehmann or Ives toys. If you want to collect battery toys, look for the things I mentioned earlier: toys in excellent condition with an interesting action and subject matter.

Another common mistake made in the battery toy field is attaching importance to age. While it may be important if a coin or stamp is from one year or another, you shouldn't worry about age as far as battery toys are concerned. I've actually been at auctions where a rusty, incomplete toy sold for more than a mint-in-box example of the same toy. When the purchaser of the beat up example was asked why they preferred it to the mint toy they answered (with a straight face), "Because it's older". While these people may be wonderful parents and kind to animals, they don't know much about battery toys. Many people think that simply because a toy is older it follows that it's more valuable. There's only one thing I can say about this belief...it's wrong. Most of the Japanese battery-operated toys were made between the mid 1950's and the late 1960's. It doesn't make much difference what specific year. Many of the remote control dogs that have little value were produced much earlier than most of the robots and astronauts, yet it would take a truckload of the dogs to equal one Mr. Atomic.

Another thing to look for while collecting these toys is what I'll call crossovers. By that I mean toys that appeal to more than one group of collectors. The Mickey Magician is a perfect example. It is desired as both a battery toy and a comic character toy. Another good example is the Santa At The Desk Bank. This toy has three different groups of collectors looking for it...Santa collectors, mechanical bank collectors, and battery toy collectors. Because these crossover toys are sought after by more collectors, they are more valuable than they would be if only one group was looking for them.

Why are battery toys becoming so collectible today? One reason may be that the children who grew up with them are becoming nostalgic. I know I have many fond memories of my Great Garloo. I got it for Christmas when I was ten years old, and it was my favorite toy. When I first became involved with toy collecting, I found I had more fun looking for a Great Garloo than any other toy.

Another possibility is that the parents who bought these toys for their children are becoming nostalgic. After all, if you think about it, battery toys were probably designed with grown-ups in mind, because they were the ones doing the buying. I can imagine an adult in a toy store twenty five years ago seeing a Barber Bear being demonstrated and thinking, "I'm sure Junior would love that." So the toy would be purchased. Junior would have had no say in the matter at all.

Another reason battery toys are more desirable today is that as the number of collectors increases, the number of toys available to these collectors is limited. Once purchased, very few battery toys survived.

When Junior received his battery toy for Christmas, he probably enjoyed it at first. But how long can you expect a child to watch a toy repeat the same action over and over again? Most battery toys were made to be watched, while children like to pick up and play with their toys. These toys were often very fragile, and most children couldn't understand that they weren't supposed to pick the toy up by its head or hit it with their new baseball bat. They also consumed batteries at an alarming rate. (Remember, this was before the days of Duracells and the Energizer).

This combination of factors often resulted in a quick trip into the garbage for the battery toy (usually soon after Christmas). The luckier ones were stuck away in the attic or basement to be thrown away the following April during Spring cleaning. When you look at it in this light, it isn't surprising that few of these wonderful toys survived. This scarcity only adds to their value as collectibles.

As a general rule, if a toy is mostly tin and made in Japan, it is collectible. If it is a plush toy such as a bear or other animal, check the feet or battery box. If these are tin, then this toy is also a good collectible. There are certain tin Japanese toys that are not particularly valuable, and certain plastic ones that are, but these will be discussed later.

There are still tin toys being made today, but almost all of these come from China, Korea, or Taiwan. These toys might be collected in the future, but they are not particularly sought after now. The Japanese still make a few battery toys today (mostly robots), but most of these are completely or predominantly plastic. Towards the back of the book I've included a chart to try to give you an idea of which battery toys are most desirable to collectors. This can be a useful guide for those just beginning in this hobby. In the chart I've listed some of the main problems you will probably have with individual toys (things like missing parts or common mechanical failings). Whether you buy your toys at toy shows, flea markets, at auctions, antique shops, or through the mail, having a general idea of what to look for, using this chart as a reference, and keeping in mind the importance of condition, you may save yourself from the numerous mistakes so many of us make as beginning collectors.

In conclusion, let me welcome all the new collectors who are interested in these modern day automata. Whether you're collecting for fun or profit, I can only hope that battery toys bring you as many hours of pleasure as they have brought me.

CARE AND REPAIR

Part of the challenge and fun of collecting battery operated toys is to find and keep them in good working order. This is not always an easy thing to do. When you find them in working order, half the battle is won. However you should avoid certain things to keep them working. Like a car, most battery toys perform best when used fairly regularly. This doesn't mean you have to run each toy every day, but they should be allowed to work for a few minutes every few months. This prevents the mechanisms from freezing up. If for any reason the toy should stop working, never force parts by hand. This will very rarely help matters, and will often cause severe trouble in a toy that had a very simple problem.

With such toys as the Bubble Blowing Popeye, you may be tempted to actually let him blow bubbles, and it would probably be fun to take your tin Nautilus Submarine into the tub with you too, but there is a simple equation that you should consider before doing these things:

Tin toys + liquids = Rusty tin toys

If you want your toys to stay in good condition, avoid using them with water or soap bubble solution.

It's also a good idea to keep them out of direct sunlight. The materials used to make their fur and clothing are not colorfast, and will fade quickly under bright light.

Although today's batteries don't leak as often as they used to, you should always remove them when you're finished playing with the toy. It's better to be safe than sorry.

Otherwise, just use common sense. Try not to drop your toys from any great heights. Don't play with them in the rain. Discourage your cat from sharpening his claws on them, etc.

When you purchase a toy that is not working, that is where the challenge comes in. It would be impossible for me to list all of the possible problems that a battery toy could have, but I will try to explain the most common ones.

Generally when a toy is bought "as is", it does nothing at all. Strangely enough, this is usually much easier to remedy than the problem of the toy that is functioning partially. When you do get a toy that does nothing, the first thing to check is the battery case.

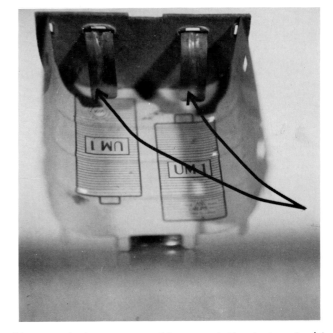

Closeup of a battery case. (Arrow pointing to terminals).

Check to make sure:
A - The batteries are inserted correctly.
B - The battery terminal contacts are free of rust and corrosion.
C - The battery terminals are making contact with both ends of the battery.
D - The batteries are not dead.

If the problem is A or D then I'm sure that even the least mechanically inclinded can figure out what should be done. If the terminals don't seem to be clean and shiny (B), take a piece of fine sandpaper or an emory board and gently clean the terminal contacts to remove any corrosion. If the contacts are not touching both ends of the battery, remove the battery and bend the contacts out by hand. Reinsert your batteries, and if the toy is still not functioning, you can safely assume that the battery case is not the problem.

When these battery toys were first manufactured, they were lubricated at the factories to insure smooth operation. This brings us to the second common cause of a battery toy not working. Many toys sat in a warehouse for twenty years or more without being touched. This prolonged inactivity caused the oil originally used to gradually thicken and harden. Instead of lubricating, it actually prevents the gears from moving at all.

When you have a spoiled child who will simply not do what you want him to do, a few smacks on the rear end will sometimes do wonders. This also holds true for many battery toys. Holding the toy firmly and giving it a few moderate hits can loosen that oil and allow the toy to resume normal operations.

Moderation is the key here. You certainly don't want to get carried away and abuse the poor toy. Also there are certain toys you don't ever want to try this with at all. This tactic should be avoided with toys with complex mechanical parts such as electro magnets (Fishing Bears, Mickey and Fox Magicians, etc.), die cast gears (High Jinx, Frankenstein, Good Time Charlie, Roulette Man, etc.), any unusually fragile toys (Santa On Globe, Space Explorer Robot, Jungle Trio, Lady Pup Gardener, etc.) or any other toy that is very valuable, rare, or for any reason difficult to replace. It can't do any harm to a Drinking Rabbit, Piggy Chef, Blacksmith Bear, or a majority of other battery toys. These toys are sturdier than they look. Just use common sense, and when in doubt, try something else first.

Another way to free "frozen" toys is to give them a sudden jolt of extra power. Go to any electronic store and purchase a battery holder. This is a plastic box with battery terminals and two wires extending from it. One wire will be positive, the other negative. They can be obtained to hold either two or four batteries in AA, C or D sizes. The one that holds four D batteries will give you the most use. Fill it with fresh batteries and touch the positive wire to the positive terminal of the toy and the negative wire to the negative terminal.

If this doesn't work you can try one last method. Try to lift or separate the clothes or fur, or on robots look where the legs go into the body. See if you can find a gear that can be reached either by a finger or a small screwdriver and try to gently spin the gear by hand. If a small piece of cloth or dust is stuck between the teeth of the gears, this method will loosen it and allow normal operation. If the gear does not turn fairly easily, do not force it or you will risk serious damage.

If the toy has been repaired by any of the methods described so far you can consider yourself fortunate. You didn't have to disassemble the toy. If you do have to take a toy apart, do so very carefully. Do not bend the small tabs that hold the toy together any more than necessary. They are fragile and may break.

When you have exposed the mechanism of the toy, check to see that all the wires are attached at both ends. If you do find a loose wire, that is probably your problem. You'll need a soldering gun and some solder to repair it. Try to locate the spot where the wire belongs. There should be at least two wires going to each of these parts:

1 - Battery box or remote control
2 - Motor
3 - On/Off switch
4 - Any light or smoke mechanism

If the wiring seems to be okay, the problem could be a jammed gear, a burned out motor, or any number of other things. Your easiest method of repairing it would be to find someone else to do it for you.

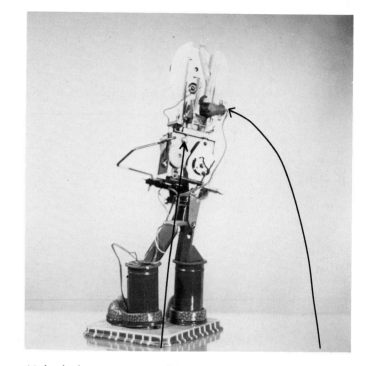

Naked battery toy. (Arrows pointing to smoke mechanism and pinion gear).

Two different battery operated motors:
On left: *With brass pinion gear.*
On right: *With plastic pinion gear.* (Arrows pointing to pinion gear.

Closeup of a smoke mechanism.

Moving on to toys that work partially, but don't do what they were intended to do: a common problem, especially with toys made in the mid to late 1960's, is the plastic pinion gear. The disease is disgnosed by looking for the following symptom...when the patient is turned on, he or she will make a whirring noise but do nothing. This is caused by a defect in the pinion gear, a very small gear that is attached directly to the motor. In earlier toys, this gear was made of brass, but in some later toys, plastic was used, and almost without fail, these plastic gears cracked and no longer function. The repair is fairly simple. Once the toy is apart, just remove the offending plastic gear and replace it with a brass one. You may be able to obtain these gears from a local machine shop, or you can get them from junkers.

You can often find rusty, broken toys at flea markets for a few dollars. Although they don't have any value as collectible toys, they are well worth the investment because they can be taken apart and "stripped" of all usable parts (gears, lights, smoke mechanisms, etc.).

One part of many battery toys that never ceases to amaze people is the smoke mechanism. It is an inch-long, round, gray object that holds a coiled wire, surrounded by an oil-soaked wad of cotton. It works along the same principle as a light bulb except instead of producing light it produces heat. The heat burns the oil and that produces the smoke that is blown out of the mouth, ears or gun of the toy in question. If the toy is not smoking, first make sure that your batteries are fresh. Next, try putting a drop (not too much) of oil into the hole the smoke should be coming from. Let the toy run for a few minutes and it may begin smoking. If not, I mentioned that smoke mechanisms are similar to light bulbs, and like light bulbs, they sometimes burn out. A burned out smoke mechanism must be replaced, just as the pinion gear was.

I've tried to give you a few tips on common repairs made on battery toys. If you enjoy tinkering, with a little practice you will soon be able to spot and repair many of the things mentioned here, as well as some of the more complex defects sometimes encountered.

If you are not mechanically inclined or don't have the desire to do any repair work, then either find a toy repair person you can trust, or avoid buying toys that don't work.

Quite a few battery toys have a specific defect that is found in some or all examples of that toy. For example, High Jinx the Clown with Monkey has a die cast (as opposed to steel or brass) gear which controls the lifting of the monkey into the air. Unfortunately, this gear could not take the tremendous strain placed on it by the lifting action, and consequently many of them cracked. Therefore, there are quite a few High Jinx out there that work partially, but will not lift the monkey. For warnings about problems of this kind, refer to the chart toward the back of the book. If a toy has a problem that is common to many of its kind, I will mention it there, and you will know what to look for when buying or repairing that toy.

I realize that I've hardly scratched the surface of toy repair, but it is not a subject that can be covered in one chapter. If you really want to learn how to repair battery operated toys the best method is probably still trial and error. This can be very frustrating at times, but the satisfaction of knowing that you took a broken toy and made it work properly again makes it all worthwhile.

THE TOYS

While putting this book together, I had to limit the toys that were to be included. I certainly couldn't include all of the thousands of different battery toys produced over the last thirty years. Time, space and availability made this impossible.

There are two major groups of toys in the world of battery operated toys, figurals (robots, animals, people etc.) and vehicles (cars, planes, trucks, ships etc.). I've tried to cover the figural battery toys as completely as possible. Since I've collected the figurals for ten years, and many of my friends were kind enough to allow me access to their collections, I feel that I've included most of the unique and more desirable toys in this area.

Unfortunately, my knowledge of the other main group, vehicles, is limited to say the least. I have little contact with vehicle collectors, and I had a difficult time putting this part of the book together. Mr. Dale Kelley was kind enough to help me by photographing part of his collection, and giving me the information necessary to do the section on cars.

In the descriptions of each toy pictured on the following pages, I've given the materials of which the toy is constructed (tin, cloth, plastic, rubber, plush, etc.) and a brief explanation of its actions. This can be helpful if you have a toy that is not working properly. I've also included the country of origin if the toy was *not* made in Japan.

The descriptions may include certain terms with which you may not be familiar. Some of the terms used and their meanings are as follows:

Remote Control: A tin or plastic box attached to the toy by wires. It has two functions, to hold the batteries and operate the toy.

Bump And Go Action: Causes a toy to automatically turn and move in another direction when it encounters an obstacle.

Non-Fall Action: Prevents a toy from falling off a surface. When it reaches an edge, it turns and moves away.

Stop And Go Action: The toy will move for a specific length of time, stop automatically, then resume operation.

For further information on each toy, such as size, desirability, and common problems, refer to the chart at the back of the book.

When I discuss variations in toys, I can be referring to a number of different things. Two toys can have the same action with different figures performing it, as is the case with 15E and 15F, the Busy Housekeepers. Toys can have the same action with the same figure performing the action, but have differences in color or detail, as with 14A and 14B, the Rock 'N' Roll Monkeys. Toys can also be similar in appearance but have completely different actions, such as 20A and 20B, the Fox Magicians.

Variations were a useful tool to make old toys seem like something completely different. It's easy to see how the Japanese were able to keep coming up with new variations each year. Their mechanisms were easily adaptable, so all that was needed was a new head or different lithograph on the toy, and the words "all new" printed on the box.

Using nothing but long-nosed pliers, a screwdriver, and a bunch of Bartender junkers, I was able to produce seven completely different battery operated toys. Two are pictured here. On the left is the original Charlie Weaver Bartender. Next comes the Great Illusionist, a magician who shakes and points a lighted magic wand as a rabbit pops out of his hat. He then lifts his handkerchief to reveal a crystal ball. Inside the ball, a face lights up. The final variation shown is the Mad Doctor (before and after). A scientist shakes up a beaker, and pours the contents into a glass. The glass smokes. He drinks from the glass, the normal face is ejected and his "Mr. Hyde" face is revealed.

The ideas for designing toy mechanisms are limitless, and once conceived, almost any idea can be put into effect. It seems that an imagination was the most important ingredient in the manufacture of battery-toys.

From left to right: *Charlie Weaver Bartender, Great Illusionist, Dr. Jeckyl and Mr. Hyde.*

A   B   C

D   E   F   G

The reference numbers for each of the toys pictured in this book (1A, 1B, 2A, 2B, 2C, etc.) are included for easy identification and cross reference with the desirability chart in the back of the book.

The numbers refer to the photo number while the letters correspond to the position of each toy in the photo. The letters start from the top row left and end on the bottom row right as shown in this example:

16

ANIMALS

This is probably the largest group of figural battery toys. I'll break this group down even further into two sub-species: the normal animals and the personified animals. The normal animal does exactly what he does in real life (walking, barking dogs, quacking ducks, etc.). The personified animal is busy doing something he could never do in real life, something normally associated with people (reading bear, monkey playing guitar, etc.). The second group is more popular with collectors, and therefore will be covered more fully in this chapter.

1A. **Buttons the Dog:** Plush dog on a tin base has eight buttons that control eight different actions. These actions can be performed individually or in any combination and include: moving paw, tail, head, eyes and mouth. Has barking sound.

1B. **Dancing Merry Chimp:** A recent toy (late 70's), yet already collectible. Plush monkey on a tin base has four buttons that control the dancing, swaying, clapping, moving eyes, ears and mouth. Actions performed alone or together.

2A. **Talking Parrot:** Plush bird on a tin base. Head turns, wings and tail flap, eyes light, and a tape recorder in the perch records and repeats whatever you say. Unique action.

2B. **Pretty Peggy Parrot:** Similar to the Talking Parrot minus the tape recorder feature. This parrot squawks.

2C. **Flutterbirds:** Another unusual toy has two plush birds that fly up and down above a tin birdhouse as a third bird moves and chirps in the door. Light on the birdhouse lights.

18

3A. **Circus Elephant:** Remote control elephant walks while blowing a ball above his trunk.

3B. **Jolly Penguin:** Remote control penguin waddles forward with moving wings and head.

3C. **Chippy the Chipmunk:** Remote control plush animal with a nut in his mouth runs with moving feet and lighting eyes. He rises on his hind legs and begs.

3D.
3E.
3F. **Remote Control Dogs:** There must be more than fifty different varieties of these dogs. Most of them bark, walk or run with moving legs, tail, head and opening mouth. The eyes usually light.

4A. **Rooster:** Tin bird with cloth tail walks with moving head and "rooster sound".

4B.

4C. **Singing Birds:** Two different versions with similar actions. The birds sing realistically as they move their heads and tails.

4D. **Duck:** Plush fowl with rubber feet and tin beak quacks, moves its head and wings as its eyes light. Bump and go action.

4E. **Worried Mother Duck:** Mostly tin Mama duck rolls, quacks and occasionally turns around to make sure her baby is still following her.

5A. **Pet Turtle:** Tin turtle with vinyl legs and tail. When a string extending from his shell is pulled, he moves with bump and go action. When it is pulled again, his feet and head move, and he makes a growling sound. Eyes also light.

5B. **Alley the Alligator:** Beautifully made plush and vinyl remote control toy. Walks, growls and swings his tail in a very real manner.

5C. **Circus Lion:** Plush lion on a tin base stands up thrashing his paws, and growls when you touch his blanket with the magic wand. Touch the other side of the blanket and he stops.

5D. **Bengal Tiger:** Remote control plush tiger. Walks with real stalking action and growls.

21

6A. **Gorilla:** Plush and tin remote-control ape walks forward leaning on his knuckles. His eyes light and his mouth opens.

6B. **Yeti-The Abominable Snowman:** A plush and tin remote control toy. He walks, stops, raises his arms and lets out the most amazing screech you'll ever want to hear. Nice litho on the remote control.

6C. **Gorilla:** An albino gorilla walks, moves arms and mouth, growls and his eyes light. Has one of the nicest lithoed remote controls (shown) of the figural battery operated toys.

6D. **Roaring Gorilla:** A mostly tin target game. When you shoot the gorilla in the chest with the gun provided, he raises his arms and roars. The bottom half of the box opens to form a jungle background.

7A. **Caterpillar:** Remote control plush and tin caterpillar inches itself forward as its eyes light.

7B. **Pat the Roaring Elephant:** Plush elephant walks, raises her trunk and roars as her baby follows behind her.

7C. **Baby Bertha:** Vinyl circus elephant on a tin base stands up and shoots a stream of water out of her trunk.

8A. **Balloon Blowing Monkey:** Plush monkey on a tin base. He kicks his feet, raises the balloon to his mouth and actually inflates it. Eyes also light.

8B.

8C. **Balloon Blowing Teddy:** Two color variations with the same action as the Balloon Blowing Monkey.

8D.

8E. **Grandpa Bear:** Plush bear in a tin rocker smokes his lighting pipe and exhales smoke as he rocks in his chair. Shown in the two color variations.

9A. **Blacksmith Bear:** Plush bear on a tin base holds a horseshoe over a forge, moves it over to his anvil and strikes it with his mallet. Eyes, anvil and forge light.

9B. **Reading Bear:** Plush bear with lighting eyes sits on a tin base. He turns the pages of a book as if reading.

9C. **Dentist Bear:** Plush and tin toy features a dentist drilling on his young patient. He stops and the young bear spits. Drill lights and both heads move.

9D. **Barber Bear:** From the same series as the Dentist Bear. He cuts the hair of his young customer, the baby bear looks in the mirror and then kicks his feet and moves his arms to show his approval.

9E. **Beauty Parlor Bear:** Similar action to Barber Bear except the beautician holds a curler instead of scissors.

These three toys comprise one of the most popular series of figural battery toys made.

25

10.A.
Barney Drumming Bear: Plush and tin remote control bear walks, turns head and plays his drum as his eyes light.

10B.
Peter Drumming Rabbit: Plush and tin remote control rabbit. Same action as Barney.

10C.
Musical Bear: This guy not only plays the drum, but toots his own horn as well. Plush and tin, remote control.

10D.
Drumming Bear: Plush and tin remote control bear plays drum and cymbals.

10E.
Musical Jackal: This sure looks like a monkey to me, but the box says "jackal". His eyes light, he sways from side to side, turns his head and plays the xylophone. Plush and tin, remote control.

10F.
Musical Bear: This toy has the same action as the Musical Jackal.

11A.
Hoopy the Fishing Duck: Plush and tin with rubber feet. He lifts his pole out of a pond with a fish on the line. Reaching down, he grabs the fish, throws it into his basket, and quacks. Eyes also light.
11B.
11C.
Fishing Bear: Both the Panda bear and Polar bear have the same action as the Fishing Duck except they laugh instead of quacking. There is also a brown and white spotted variation.

11D.
Piggy Cook: Tin, vinyl, and cloth chef sways while holding a frying pan over a lighted stove. He seasons and finally flips a ham and egg omelet.
11E.
Doggy Chef: Same action as the Pig Chef with the addition of moving eyes and ears that perk up (also he prefers a hamburger). Best action of the chef series.
11F.
Bear Chef: Same action as Pig Chef plus he turns his head.

27

12A.

12B. **Telephone Bear:** Two different versions of the same great toy. He's busy writing when the phone rings. He answers it, makes an extremely cute speaking sound, and nods his head. Tin and plush.

12C. **Vip Busy Boss Bear:** With this toy you have to dial the large phone to start the action. The bear's phone rings and lights, he picks it up and starts writing. Action stops automatically until you call again. Plush and cloth bear, tin desk and phone.

12D. **Bear Cashier:** This plush bear doesn't write at all, but does do math problems on its adding machine until the phone rings. Answers phone, head moves. Tin desk, phone and adding machine. There is also a rabbit variation.

13A. **Music Hall:** Tin base and piano, plush dog. The dog's movements are very simple, but the piano plays an actual song.

13B.

13C. **Jolly Pianist:** Although these toys only make a clanging sound, they have better action as the dogs move their eyes, arms, and heads, and the keys of the piano really move. Plush dogs with tin base and piano.

13D. **Musical Bulldog:** Again, a very simple action (only the dog's arms move), but on a very impressive looking toy. The dog's tin cigar lights, and he blows out smoke. Tin, cloth and plush.

14A.
14B. **Rock 'N' Roll Monkey:** Two different versions: one has a cloth face, the other vinyl. The toy is tin, plastic and cloth. The monkey strums his guitar, sways from side to side, stomps his foot, and seems to sing into the lighted microphone. The monkey's hand striking the strings makes the "music".
14C.
14D. **Bongo Monkey:** Plush monkey with a vinyl face sits on a tin base. Body moves from side to side as he beats the drums with his hands. One version has lighting eyes.

15A.
15B.
Sneezing Bear: Plush bear on a tin base leans back, sneezes and wipes his nose with a tissue. Eyes light.
15C.
Knitting Grandma: Plush cat on tin base knits with moving hands, head and lighted eyes.
15D.
Monkey Artist: Plush monkey on tin base rubs his brush on the palette then moves it down to work on his painting. Head moves and painting and palette light.

15E.
15F.
Busy Housekeepers: Plush rabbit and bear move forward and back and turn their heads as if really vacuuming. The rabbit is shown using an upright that lights. The bear uses a canister vacuum. There are other variations.

31

16A. **Telephone Rabbit:** Plush rabbit in a tin rocking chair. As he rocks, the phone rings. He brings the receiver to his ear, moves his lips and makes a chattering sound.

16B.

16C. **Telephone Bear:** These have the same action as the rabbit except they sit on stationary bases. One has a stick phone, while the other has a lighted table phone.

16D. **Papa Bear:** Plush bear in a tin rocker drinks and reads as he rocks in his chair. Eyes also light.

16E. **Birdwatcher Bear:** Plush bear on a tin base. A singing bird flies back and forth as the bear moves his head watching it.

16F. **Mother Bear:** Plush bear in a tin rocking chair rocks as she moves her hands in a knitting motion.

All of these bubble blowing toys have similar actions. They dunk a wand into a soapie bubble solution, lift it to their mouths, and blow bubbles.

17A. **Bubble Blowing Elephant:** Tin base, plush elephant, plastic water bucket.

17B. **Bubble Blowing Rabbit:** Mostly tin.

17C. **Bubble Blowing Kangaroo:** Tin with rubber ears.

17D. **Bubbles Washing Bear:** Plush bear on tin base moves up and down as if scrubbing laundry while bubbles come from the wash basin.

17E. **Bubble Blowing Monkey:** Plush and tin with lighting eyes.

17F. **Bubble Blowing Dog:** Plush and tin.

18A. **Royal Cub:** A plush bear pushes a tin carriage. As she walks along, the baby lifts a bottle to his mouth and makes a crying sound.

18B. **Rabbit Carriage:** Same action as Royal Cub except this baby holds a carrot.

18C. **Hungry Baby Bear:** Plush and tin. A mama bear with moving head, and eyes that open and close, feeds her baby with a milk bottle. When she pulls the bottle away, the baby kicks its arms and legs and cries.

18D. **Hungry Baby Pup:** Has same action as Hungry Baby Bear.

18E. **Spanking Bear:** A cute variation of the Hungry Baby Bear. The mother gives the baby a few whacks on the rear end, causing the baby to kick its arms and legs and cry. Mother's head moves, and her eyes open and close.

19A.
19B. **Playful Dog:** Both toys have similar actions. One dog moves up and down and side to side, barking at a mouse hidden in a log. The mouse sticks his head out of one side and then the other. The other dog is playing with a wiggling caterpillar. Both dogs are plush on tin bases.

19C.
19D. **Lion Target Game and Bubble Blowing Lion:** Here we see how the Japanese used the same parts to make two different toys. Although the shapes are the same, the litho and mechanisms are very different. Lion target game comes with a plastic dart gun. When shot with a dart, the lion moves his head and roars. The bubble blowing lion blows bubbles from his mouth. Both lions have eyes that light.

20A.

20B. **Bear Target Game and Bubble Blowing Bear:** Another example of two related toys with different actions. The bear target game turns his head and beats a drum when shot with the provided pistol. The bubble blower moves his head and arms, lifts a lighting pipe to his mouth and blows out bubbles. Both bears have lighted eyes.

20C. **Mr. Fox Magician:** Tin and plush toy features a fox who lifts his hat to reveal a rabbit, points to it, lifts the hat again and the rabbit is gone.

20D. **Mr. Fox Magician - Bubble Blower:** Similar to above except bubbles come from under the hat instead of a disappearing rabbit.

21A.
21B.
21C. **Picnic Bunny:** Three color variations of this plush toy on a tin base. The rabbit with lighted eyes actually pours water from a bottle to its cup and appears to drink it. The water runs through a tube from the cup back to the bottle, and the action is repeated.

21D. **Drinking Bear**

21E. **Drinking Monkey**

21F. **Drinking Panda Bear**

The above three toys are variations of the Picnic Bunny toy.

Drumming Animal One Man Bands

Six versions of the popular drumming toy. All have lighted eyes and moving heads. The figures beat on the drums and cymbals with their hands and feet.

22A. **Mambo the Drumming Elephant**

22B. **Dandy the Drumming Dog**

22C. **Daisy the Drumming Duck**

22D. **Peter the Drumming Rabbit**

22E. **Dalmatian One Man Band**

22F. **Chimpy the Drumming Monkey**

23A. **Shoemaker Bear:** Plush bear on tin base beats on a boot with his hammer while smoking a pipe and shaking his head.

23B. **Shoeshine Monkey:** Plush chimp on a tin base turns the boot in his hand as he buffs it with a brush. His pipe lights.

23C. **Shoeshine Bear:** Same action as the monkey.

All plush and tin remote control figures walk, lift the lighting pipe to their mouths and exhale smoke.

23D. **Smoking Elephant**

23E. **Mr. Mc Pooch**

23F. **Smoking Papa Bear**

23G. **Smoking Rabbit**

24A. **Bobby the Drinking Bear:** Remote control plush and tin bear walks carrying a tray. He pours and drinks. Eyes light.

24B.

24C. **Jocko the Drinking Monkey:** tin monkey pours a drink and really pours it into his mouth and drinks it. Liquid comes back into the bottle and the action is repeated. Eyes light. Two versions show casual and formal dress.

24D.

24E. **Drinking Dog:** Both versions are plush dogs on tin bases. They pour and then lift a drink to their mouths. Both have lighted eyes.

24F. **Maxwell Coffee-Loving Bear:** Plush bear on a tin base holds a coffee pot that lights up and smokes from the spout. He seems to pour and drink the coffee.

25A. **Traveler Bear:** Plush and tin remote control bear with a suitcase. He walks with moving legs and head, and has lighted eyes.

25B. **Sleeping Baby Bear:** Plush bear in a tin bed. The hands move on the alarm clock and the alarm goes off. The bear sits up in bed, stretches his arms, opens his mouth, closes his eyes and makes a yawning sound...then goes back to sleep.

25C. **Teddy the Artist:** Plush bear on tin base. He moves his head, closes his eyes and draws any one of nine different pictures. Nine interchangable picture templates are included.

25D. **Susie the Cashier Bear:** Plush bear on tin base rings up items on her cash register as she pushes them along on the moving conveyor belt. Great action.

26A. **Teddy Go Cart:** A plush bear pulls a tin cart behind him. As he moves along, the cart gets heavier and lifts the crying bear into the air. His feet kick the air, and he struggles to pull the cart again.

26B. **Cappy the Baggage Porter:** Plush dog pulls a tin cart, turning his head as he goes. He has lighted eyes.

26C. **Chimp and Pup Railcar:** Mostly tin toy. The animals (with lighted, blinking eyes) pump up and down as their handcar moves forward.

26D. **Penguin on Tricycle:** Remote control tin penguin peddles his tricycle around in a circle as he opens his mouth and makes a quacking sound. Light on tricycle works.

27A.   **Popcorn Vendor Bear:** Plush bear rides a tin cart. As he peddles, he sways, the umbrella on the cart spins, and the popcorn pops. There is also a rabbit version of this toy.

27B.   **Mac The Turtle:** Tin, cloth, and vinyl figure walks along pushing a large tin whiskey barrel. As he goes, he slips and ends up on top of the barrel. Head lights.

27C.   **Jolly Bear Peanut Vendor:** Plush bear pushes a smoking tin cart. The interior of the cart lights up as the peanuts bounce around inside.

27D.   **Popcorn Vendor Duck:** Mostly tin toy. Duck moves along pushing a popcorn cart, as corn pops inside.

28A.
Yum Yum Kitty: Plush cat on a tin base. She lifts a fish to her opening mouth, makes chewing sounds and then rubs her stomach. Eyes light.

28B.
Jolly Bambino: Plush and tin monkey pours a piece of candy from a can, throws it into his mouth, kicks his feet, then eats another piece.

28C.
Picnic Monkey: Plush monkey on a tin base alternately eats a banana and drinks from a can of soda. He gradually leans backwards until his stomach suddenly bloats out as if he has eaten too much. He squeaks and

pats his stomach until it goes down and he starts eating again.

28D.
Suzette the Eating Monkey: Mostly tin toy. A monkey cuts pieces of steak with her knife. She picks it up with her fork, drops it into her mouth, chews and swallows it, and starts cutting again. Eyes also move.

28E.
Hungry Cat: Plush cat on tin base with plastic fishbowl. When bowl is filled with water, goldfish swim around trying to avoid the swinging paws of the cat. The cat's eyes light up and its tail swings realistically.

29A.
Professor Owl: Mostly tin toy. An owl wearing a mortarboard turns and points to the blackboard, which pictures various objects followed by their names. Pictures rotate, featuring animals, fruits, etc. Two picture plates are included.
29B.
Ball Playing Bear: Tin and celluloid toy. Celluloid balls travel up a coil and drop through a hoop held by the bear. Bear's head nods, a goose turns and honks, and an umbrella spins overhead.

29C.
Jungle Trio: A tin, vinyl and rubber toy. It features one monkey who beats a drum as another plays the cymbals and an elephant blows a whistle with his trunk.
29D.
Feeding Birdwatcher: Plush and tin toy. A mother bird with a worm in her beak flies from her branch to a nest where three babies are waiting. The babies open and close their mouths and chirp loudly as the mama feeds them.

30A. **Saxophone Monkey:** Plush monkey on a tin base thrusts his body forward while tooting on the sax. He beats a drum with one foot while trying to swat a bee flying near his ear with the other.

30B. **Trumpet Monkey:** Same as above except he toots a horn instead of the sax and rings a bell with his right foot instead of playing a drum.

30C. **Accordion Bear:** Plush and tin bear with lighted eyes sways back and forth while turning his head and playing the accordion. The remote control is in the shape of a microphone. Great toy.

30D. **Bruno the Accordion Bear:** A remote control plush bear with lighted eyes dances sideways while playing the accordion.

31A.
Frankie the Rollerskating Monkey: Remote control plush monkey skates with incredibly realistic head, arm and leg movements. Also comes in a skiing version.
31B.
Big John: Plastic and tin monkey beats on the large drum while whistling. This is one of the later Japanese battery toys.
31C.
Yo-Yo Monkey: Plush monkey with vinyl face sways from side to side while spinning a yo-yo between his hands.

31D.
Friendly Jocko: Very unusual tin, cloth and vinyl toy. The monkey's tail acts as a clamp to hold the remote control toy on a person's arm or shoulder. Comes with various accessories (cymbals, cup) that can be attached to the monkey. He chatters with great facial movements, tips his hat and plays the cymbals or shakes a cup.
31E.
Crapshooting Monkey: Plush, vinyl and tin toy. The monkey first shakes up his dice, then throws them out of the dice cup.

32A. **Bunny Magician:** Plush and tin rabbit turns his head and tips his hat while performing a magic card trick.

32B. **Windy:** Plush elephant on a tin base waves her feet in the air while either spinning an umbrella above her trunk or blowing a ball in the air.

32C. **Lady Pup Gardener:** Tin and cloth toy. Dog bends forward and waters her flower. She leans back and blinks as the flower petals open and the inside of the flower lights.

32D. **Tricky Dog House:** Plush dog in a tin house. The house rolls around as the dog suddenly pops out of the door and barks.

32E. **Ball Playing Dog:** This plush and tin toy has one of the dullest actions of all the figurals. When you throw a ball at his raquet, he hits it back to you and lowers his raquet to prepare for the next throw.

33A. **Teddy the Boxing Bear:** Plush and tin toy. The bear moves his body forward and backward while swinging wildly at the punching bag. Head and eyes also move.

33B. **Jolly Bear:** Tin and cloth remote control bear walks and plays a drum. Bear has lighted eyes.

33C. **Cine Bear:** Plush and tin. The bear raises the camera up to his lighted eyes, and plastic bloodworms are shot from the lens. Bizarre.

33D. **Shoeshine Bear:** Plush bear on a tin base smokes a lighting pipe. He lifts his legs up to shine his shoes with the brushes he holds in his hands.

33E. **Shooting Bear:** Remote control plush and tin bear with lighted eyes walks forward, lifts the gun up, and closes one eye to help his aim. He shoots, and smoke comes from the gun barrel.

34A.
Teddy Bear Swing: Plush bear does acrobatics on a tin high bar. Very realistic movements, as he can do forward and backward flips.
34B.
Hy Que Monkey: This amazing plush, tin and vinyl toy goes through the Hear No Evil, See No Evil, Speak No Evil routine, first covering his mouth, then his eyes, and finally his ears. All the time he chatters and blows smoke from his ears. You start the action by pressing the palm of one of his hands.

35A.
Monkey Car: Plush monkey on a tin car. The monkey pumps the handcar, causing it to roll. A very early battery toy.

35B.
Trumpet Playing Rabbit: Plush figure on a tin base. The rabbit blows the horn while ringing a bell with one foot and swatting a bee with the other. A variation of the Trumpet Monkey. (30B)

35C.
Hippo Chef: Vinyl and tin toy. The hippo shakes and flips a hamburger over a lighted tin stove while seasoning it with pepper. His head also moves. Also made in an elephant version.

35D.
Popcorn Bear: Plush bear in a tin rocking chair. The bear rocks, lifts the popcorn to his mouth, and seems to chew it. Eyes light.

35E.
Drinking Cat: A plush cat on a tin base pours milk, and brings it to her mouth to drink. Her tongue darts in and out, and her eyes light.

36A. **Mr. Strongpup:** Plush dog on a tin base. Very energetic dog with lighted eyes turns his head from side to side as he works out with his weights.

36B. **Champion Weight Lifter:** Plastic and cloth. The monkey gradually works up to lifting the barbell above his head after several false starts. When he finally succeeds his face turns red.

36C. **Mighty Mike:** A plush bear with lighted eyes on a tin base. After warming up, the bear lifts his barbells over his head and they light up.

36D. **Happy Band Trio:** Plush animals on a tin base with a cardboard backdrop. A later Japanese battery toy (70's), but still a nice piece. The three animals move their arms and heads as if actually playing "Twinkle Twinkle Little Star" on their instruments.

37A. **Mischievous Monkey:** Tin and vinyl toy. A monkey holding a bone teases the bulldog until he jumps out of his house and barks loudly. The monkey jumps to the top of the tree and then slowly comes down again.

37B. **Clown and Lion:** Similar to 37A except the lion roars, sending the frightened clown up the tree.

37C. **Charm the Cobra:** Plastic and tin toy. When a flute is played (or any similar sound is made) a snake will slowly rise out of the basket, going back in when the sound stops.

37D. **Pipie the Whale:** Tin whale with rubber fins actually works in the water. As he swims along moving his tail, he shoots water from his spout.

PEOPLE

This group includes clowns (among the most colorful and popular of all battery toys); ethnic groups (Blacks, Indians, etc.); and a very interesting series of toys that were never meant for children, the bar toys. These were adult novelties, often given as gag gifts or put on home bars to amuse friends. A few of the more common examples are Charlie Weaver, Good Time Charlie, Blushing Willie, and the Crapshooter.

38A.
Funland Cup Ride: Tin and plastic carnival toy where the strange looking children ride in spinning cups under a twirling umbrella.

38B.
Serpent Charmer: Predominantly tin toy. An Indian man plays his flute to charm the snake. It appears from its basket and moves to the sound.

39A.
Calypso Joe: Remote control tin and cloth Black man walks with moving head and lighted eyes as he beats on a drum with his hands.

39B.
Nutty Nibs: Tin native continuously flips nuts (ball bearings) into his mouth and swallows them. His eyes also move. A great toy.

40A.
Major Tootie: Vinyl, cloth, and tin toy. A man dressed as a palace guard beats a drum and blows a whistle.

40B.
Mr. Traffic Policeman: Vinyl, cloth, and tin toy. A cop waves his arms and blows a whistle to stop traffic. When the light changes, the policeman turns and stops traffic in the other direction.

40C.
Shaving Sam: Plush, vinyl, and tin toy. The man's face lights up showing whiskers. He shaves using an electric shaver, turns his head to look in the mirror, and powders his face with a smoking powder puff.

40D.
Happy Miner: Tin, vinyl, and cloth toy. Remote control gnome-like man walks along pushing a wheelbarrow. His head turns and his eyes light.

40E.
Cycling Daddy: Plastic and tin toy. Man peddles a tricycle while waving and smoking a lighted pipe.

56

41A.
Playboy: Vinyl and cloth man on a tin base. He pours a drink and spins around on his bar stool after drinking it. His face lights.

41B.
Charlie Weaver Bartender: Tin, vinyl, and cloth TV personality shakes, pours, and consumes a drink. His face turns red and smoke comes from his ears. Body sways from side to side.

41C.
Good Time Charlie: Vinyl, cloth, and tin toy. A drunk sits on a garbage can under a streetlamp kicking his foot. He drinks from a flask and puffs on a cigar, blowing smoke from his mouth. Face turns red.

41D.
Crapshooter: Tin, vinyl, and cloth gambling man with a chewing motion. He shakes the dice in the cup and throws them out on the table, waves money in his hand, and sways from side to side. A much rarer version of this toy is the Roulette Man.

41E.
Chef Cook: Vinyl, cloth, and tin toy. The man sways, chews, flips an omlettte, and seasons it. The stove lights up.

42A.
Pinkee the Farmer: Mostly tin toy. Bump and go truck with moving, lighted pistons in the engine has driver who turns his head while the pigs in the back poke their heads in and out of their crate.

42B.
Kissing Couple: Tin and vinyl. Bump and go car rolls around as a celluloid bird spins and tweets on the hood. The man and woman turn to face each other as if kissing, and the man blushes.

42C.
Bubble Blowing Boy: Mostly tin toy. Boy bends over, sits up, and blows bubbles. Blue plastic cup that holds bubble solution not shown in photo.

42D.
Bubble Blowing Musician: Mostly tin. The man lowers his horn into the bubble solution, lifts it to his mouth, toots and blows bubbles.

42E.
Snake Charmer: Tin, cloth and, plastic toy. A man plays the flute as a plastic snake emerges from the basket at his feet. Smoke comes from the basket.

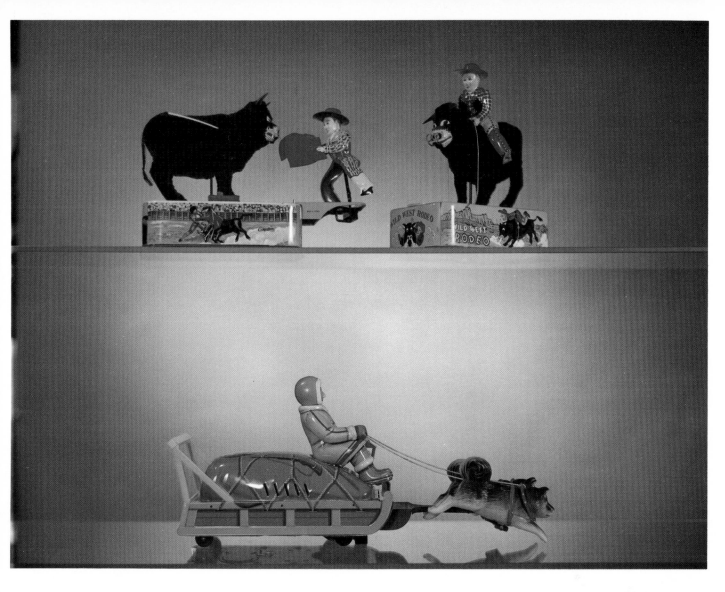

43A.
El Toro: Tin and plush toy. The bull kicks and lunges at the matador, who jumps from side to side trying to avoid him. Bull blows smoke from his nostrils.
43B.
Wild West Rodeo: Tin and plush. A tin cowboy rides on a kicking bull as the bull blows bubbles from his nose.
43C.
Dog Sled: Tin and vinyl toy. Two huskies pull an Eskimo riding on a dog sled. Has bell sound and lighted lantern. Also came in a Santa version.

44A.
Overland Stagecoach: Mostly tin toy. The horse gallops, pulling the stagecoach as the driver shakes the reins.
44B.
Cowboy on Horse: Mostly tin remote control toy. The man moves forward and back in the saddle as the horse walks.
44C.
Stagecoach: Tin and plastic toy. Two horses pull a stage with galloping motion as a man lying on top fires his rifle. Bump and go action with moving driver.

45A. **Nutty Mad Indian:** Plastic, cloth, and tin. A strange looking figure (obviously inspired by Big Daddy Roth) beats on his drum while sticking his tongue in and out and whistling. Plays an Indian rhythm.

45B. **Red Gulch Bar:** Tin, cloth, and vinyl toy. A lithographed bartender pours a drink for a Western badman. After his drink, the outlaw's face turns red, and he fires his gun.

45C. **Pistol Pete:** Tin and cloth remote control man walks, aims, and shoots his gun. The gun flashes and smoke comes out of the barrel.

45D. **Dancing Indian:** Cloth, plastic, and tin remote control toy. The Indian beats his drum, changes his facial expression, and does a sideways dance.

45E. **Two Gun Sheriff:** Cloth, plastic, and tin remote control lawman steps from side to side, changes his facial expression, and shoots his guns.

46A. **Girl with Baby Carriage:** Plastic, cloth, and tin toy. The girl walks along pushing a carriage that holds a crying baby.

46B. **Dolly Seamstress:** Tin, cloth, and vinyl toy. Girl sits at a sewing machine and operates the foot peddles while pushing a piece of material under the moving needle. As she works, a changing lighted pattern appears on the material.

46C. **Busy Secretary:** Tin and vinyl toy. The girl bangs away at a typewriter with lighted keys as she turns her head to follow what she is typing. A paper with typed words appears from the top of the typewriter.

46D. **Miss Friday Typist:** This girl types with moving hands, head and typewriter carriage. Bell rings on typewriter.

A much rarer toy in the same series as Miss Friday and the Dolly Seamstress is a telephone operator...a girl working at a telephone switchboard.

47A.
Telephone Linesman: Mostly tin toy. The man climbs up and down a telephone pole with great arm and leg movement. Light on his helmet works. The base is a Telephone Company truck.

47B.
Climbing Fireman: Mostly tin toy. A remote control fireman will walk, pushing his ladder platform until it hits a wall. He will then automatically climb up and down the ladder. Great action.

47C.
Climbing Fireman: Mostly tin. This is a simpler version of the above toy. This fireman climbs up then slides down the ladder.

47D.
Ol' Sleepy Head Rip: Tin, cloth, and vinyl toy. A spinning, tweeting bird wakes Rip Van Winkle character from his long sleep. He sits up in bed, his face lights, and he stretches and yawns before laying back down to sleep.

47E.
Smoking Grandpa: Tin and cloth. Old man sitting in a moving rocking chair lifts a lighted pipe to his mouth and exhales smoke.

48A.
Bartender: Cloth, tin, and vinyl toy. Man mixes, pours and drinks. He has a red face, swaying motion and smoke coming from his ears. A rarer version has whirling eyes.
48B.
Blushing Willie: Tin, cloth, and plastic man pours a drink and drinks it with a lighted face and whirling eyes. This toy comes in a number of variations (Capt. Blushwell, a Sheriff, etc.).
48C.
Drinking Captain: Tin, cloth, and plastic. Seaman stands under a lighted street lamp and drinks heavily until his stomach lights up and he blows smoke from it. His eyes also open and close.

48D.
Mc Gregor: Tin, cloth, and vinyl figure stands up and sits down, opens and closes his eyes, lifts a cigar to his mouth, and exhales smoke from nose and mouth. The cigar ash lights.
48E.
Puffy Morris: Tin, cloth, and vinyl seated man with moving eyes and chest smokes a real cigarette. You light the cigarette and insert it in his holder.
48F.
Pat O'Neill: Same action as Mc Gregor toy except you start his action by touching a flame to the end of his cigar.

49A. **Peppermint Twist Doll:** Vinyl and cloth girl on a tin base does a great rendition of the Twist.

49B. **My Fair Dancer:** Mostly tin toy (girl has vinyl head). A sailor girl does a jig moving her arms and legs.

49C. **Hoop Zing Girl:** Celluloid and cloth girl does gyrations as a hula hoop twirls around her.

49D. **Mr. Baseball Jr.:** Mostly tin toy. Batting machine pushes a baseball up to bat level, the player swings, and hits it. The box opens to form part of the game.

49E. **Dancing Sweethearts:** Tin and celluloid couple dance and spin as actual music comes from the base.

49F. **Shutterbug:** Mostly tin. A boy with turning head walks, lifts a camera to his face, and snaps a picture. The flash on the camera lights.

50A. **Sammy Wong:** Vinyl, tin, and cloth Chinese man pours and drinks a cup of tea. The tea pot lights and smokes.

50B. **Strutting Sam:** A tin Black man does a jig on a tin base.

50C. **Gino the Balloon Man:** Tin, plastic, and cloth Italian with moving eyes rings a bell and lifts soap solution up to his tank to blow bubbles.

50D. **Mexicali Pete:** Cloth, vinyl, and tin man moves his body while playing the drums.

50E. **Indian Joe:** Similar action to Mexicali Pete (above).

50F. **Mumbo Jumbo:** Hawaiian boy has same drumming action as Mexicali Pete (above).

51A.
Clown and Monkey Car: Tin, vinyl, plush, and plastic toy. The clown pumps the bump and go handcar as the monkey holds on to his back and waves a hat.
51B.
Clown on Unicycle: Tin, plastic, and cloth toy. A clown holding lighted balls peddles a unicycle in various directions. Great action.

52A.
Magic Man: Tin and cloth remote control clown walks, smoking a lighted pipe. He tips his hat and blows smoke rings from the top of his head.
52B.
Clown Magician: Cloth, vinyl, and tin clown sways, tips his hat and opens and closes his magical card trick. The clown's head turns and his nose lights.

51C.
Musical Comic Jumping Jeep: Plastic and tin jeep with clown driver. Rolls forward as seat and clown move up and back, music is played, and the headlights are raised and lowered. When car bumper hits an obstacle, the clown jounces up and down, using his feet to raise and turn the jeep in a new direction.
51D.
Happy Clown Car: Tin and vinyl toy. A clown with moving head drives a bump and go car with a ringing sound.
52C.
Clown Circus Car: Tin, vinyl, and cloth toy. A clown holding a mop and pail rides on an eccentrically moving circus car.
52D.
Cyclist Clown: Remote control tin clown peddles a tricycle forward and backward. Clown's head moves up and down, and his eyes move. The headlight on the tricycle lights and a bell rings.

53A.
Blinky the Clown: Beautiful cloth and tin remote control clown with a paper hat. He walks as he plays the xylophone. The clown has lighted eyes and moving head.
53B.
Bimbo the Clown: Cloth and tin remote control clown with a composition head. He walks, his nose lights, and he hits the drum.
53C.
Happy/Sad Clown: Remote control cloth, plastic, and tin clown steps from side to side while playing the xylophone and altering his expression from happy to sad.
53D.
Charlie the Drumming Clown: Tin, plastic, and cloth clown hits the snare drums and small cymbal with his drum sticks, and plays the base drum and large cymbal with his feet. As he plays, his head moves and his nose lights.
53E.
Musical Clown: Tin, cloth, and vinyl clown with moving arms and turning head plays "London Bridges" on the xylophone.

54A.

Pinky the Clown: Tin, cloth, and vinyl clown blows a whistle as he balances one ball on a rod extending from his nose while juggling another ball from hand to hand. There is also a later and larger variation called Circus Champ made of plastic and cloth.

54B.

Bingo Clown: Cloth, plastic, and tin clown walks forward; getting shorter with each step until he suddenly pops up to full size with a squeak.

54C.

Balloon Vendor: Tin, cloth and vinyl clown, with swaying body and moving mouth, holds balloons in one hand and rings a bell with the other.

54D.

Acrobat Clown: Plastic and cloth toy. The clown tumbles along doing back flips and somersaults on his hands and feet.

54E.

Rollerskating Clown: Remote control tin and cloth clown skates in different directions. Very unusual variation of the popular TPS skating figures.

55A.

High Jinx at the Circus: Cloth, tin, and plastic toy. A clown with moving head, kicking foot, and a lighted nose blows a whistle and pushes a cymbal playing chimp up in the air on an extending ladder.

55B.

Hobo Playing Accordion: Cloth, tin, and vinyl clown with moving head plays the accordion while the monkey in front of him plays the cymbals.

55C.

Yo-Yo Clown: Cloth, tin, and vinyl clown spins a yo-yo between his hands. Has life-like facial movements.

55D.

Happy the Clown Puppet Show: Tin clown with cloth outfit and vinyl face operates a tin and wood Pinnochio-like marionette. He sways and changes his facial expressions.

56A.
Laughing Clown: Plastic clown with bump and go action rolls with shaking arms. He stops, his head moves up and down, his mouth opens, he sticks out his lighted tongue, and laughs hysterically.

56B.
Dozo the Steaming Clown: Cloth, vinyl, and tin clown moves his body in a sweeping motion and rolls his eyes as smoke comes from his broom, his head and finally (as he bends over) from his rear end. He then blushes.

56C.
Ball Blowing Clown: Tin and cloth clown with bump and go action and waving arms keeps a ball suspended above him as he moves.

56D.
Happy the Violinist: Tin, cloth, and plastic. Clown moves his body and turns his head as he plays his violin. Unfortunately, he seems to need practice since his playing consists of a series of loud screeching sounds.

CHARACTER TOYS

In the pre-World War Two years, wind-up character toys were based on comic books or comic strips (Superman, Toonerville Trolley), or radio shows (Amos 'n' Andy). After the war, a new medium began to take the world by storm. This was reflected in the characters portrayed by the battery toys produced during the 50's and 60's. Almost all of them can be traced directly to television. Mr. Magoo, the Flintstones, and Tom and Jerry were all popular television cartoon show characters. The Mickey Mouse Club show introduced a whole new generation to Disney. Popeye cartoons were as popular on TV as they had been in the theater. Live action adventure shows such as Batman and Tarzan were big in the mid 60's. Smokey the Bear commercials taught children about preventing forest fires. And who can forget the immortal Topo Gigio's appearances on the Ed Sullivan Show? For better or for worse, these characters replaced the Dagwoods and Charlie McCarthys on the shelves of the post war toy stores.

Also included in this chapter is a figure who has managed to remain popular for over a century...Santa Claus. Toys based on Santa were bought as both playthings and Christmas decorations. Santa toys would have a much better chance of surviving than normal battery toys. If used as decorations, they would be out for only a week or two, and carefully packed away during the remainder of the year.

57A.
Esso Tiger: Tin and plush remote control tiger walks and growls with moving arms.

57B.
Walking Batman: Tin figure with vinyl head and cloth cape walks with swinging arms.

58A.
Smokey Bear: Remote control plush and tin bear carries a shovel over his shoulder and a lighting pipe in his hand. He walks, lifting the pipe to his mouth, and exhaling smoke.
58B.
Smokey the Bear Jeep: Mostly tin toy. Smokey drives a bump and go jeep that has a flashing light and siren sound.

58C.
Batman Car: Remote control tin car with single figure of Batman driving. Goes forward and in reverse with light in back.
58D.
Batman: Tin Batman with vinyl head and cape walks with swinging arms and a lighted insignia on his chest.
58E.
Batmobile: Tin and plastic car with both Batman and Robin riding in it. Bump and go action with flashing lights and siren sound.

59A. **Rocky:** Tin and vinyl unlicensed Flintstone toy. Caveman moves with bump and go action and swinging arms.

59B. **Fred Flintstone's Bedrock Band:** Tin, cloth, and vinyl toy. Fred plays the drums with stone mallets while operating a turtle shell cymbal with his feet.

59C. **Fred Flintsone on Dino:** Plush, vinyl, and tin toy features Fred Flintstone riding on the back of Dino the dinosaur. Dino has bump and go action, moving feet, tail, neck, and mouth, a turning head and a whistling sound.

60A. **Secret Agent Car:** The tin and plastic Aston Martin was made in two versions. The harder to find remote control version is shown. It moves with bump and go action, has machine gun bumpers, a bullet-proof shield that rises from the trunk, and a functioning ejector seat. The non-remote control Gilbert version has these actions plus a rotating license plate.

60B. **Monkeemobile:** Tin and plastic car with the figures of the rock group inside. The car moves by a friction powered motor, and plays a battery operated recording of a Monkees song.

60C. **Fred Flintstone Car:** Tin and plastic remote control Stone Age auto rolls forward and in reverse.

61A. **Topo Gigio Playing the Xylophone:** Tin, cloth, and vinyl toy. Rodent puppet made famous on the Ed Sullivan Show plays "London Bridges" on the xylophone. His head and arm move as he plays.

61B. **Topo Gigio:** Remote control cloth, tin and vinyl mouse walks with moving arms and squeaking sound.

61C. **Pinnochio Playing the Xylophone:** Same action as first toy (above). Tin, cloth, and vinyl toy.

61D. **Dennis the Menace Playing the Xylophone:** Tin, cloth, and vinyl toy. Same action as first toy (above).

73

62A. **Superman Tank:** Mostly tin toy. Rolling tank is stopped, pushed backwards, and lifted into the air by an articulated Superman figure.

62B. **Mighty Kong:** Remote control plush, tin, and vinyl toy. King Kong walks, beats his chest, opens his mouth, and roars.

62C. **Tarzan:** Tin and plastic remote control toy. Ron Ely-inspired Tarzan walks with swinging arms and roaring sound.

63A. **Disney Acrobat:** Celluloid and tin toy. Mickey does acrobatics on the high bar. Also comes in Donald Duck and Pluto versions.

63B. **Pluto Lantern:** Tin, rubber, and glass Pluto lights in stomach. Ears act as a handle.

63C. **Donald Duck:** Plush, tin and plastic Donald rolls with bump and go action. He has a wiggling tail, moving head and arms, and he makes a quacking sound.

63D. **Pluto:** Plush, plastic, tin, and rubber toy with remote control shaped like a bone. Pluto walks while wiggling his nose (that has a bee on it) and wagging his tail. He stops walking and moves his eyes and ears.

64A.
Mickey Mouse Drummer: Remote control tin and plush Mickey walks with moving head and lighted eyes as he plays his drum.
64B.
Bubble Blowing Popeye: Tin Popeye lifts a spinach can and a lighting pipe to his opening mouth and blows out bubbles.
64C.
Mickey Magician: Tin, cloth, and rubber Mickey Mouse makes a squeaking sound while pointing to his top hat and making a tin chick appear and disappear.
64D.
Smoking Popeye: Tin Popeye sits on a spinach can waving one hand while holding a lighted pipe with the other. He turns his head and blows smoke from his mouth.

76

65A.
Popeye Paddlewagon: 1970's plastic version of the popular Corgi toy. Toy rolls with non-fall action and moving figures. Made in Hong Kong.
65B.
Popeye Lantern: Mostly tin Popeye lights up from his glass belly. Arms act as the handle.
65C.
Mr. Magoo Car: Tin, plastic, and cloth auto wobbles forward as Mr. Magoo bounces up and down in the seat.
65D.
Tom and Jerry Train: One of many Tom and Jerry toys made in the late 60's. Train rolls with bump and go action, and whistle sound as Tom clangs his cymbals. Tin, vinyl, and plastic.
65E.
Mickey Mouse Handcar: Tin and vinyl toy. Mickey pumps his handcar. Bump and go action and ringing sound.
This is one of the many late 60's toys featuring Disney characters riding on various vehicles. Mickey, Donald, and others rode on handcars, trains, dune buggies, trollies etc.

66A.
Tom and Jerry Jumping Jeep: Tin and plastic toy with bump and go action. Jerry spins on a stick of dynamite in the rear.
66B.
Tom and Jerry Highway Patrol: Tin and plastic auto has bump and go action, siren sound, and flashing lights.
66C.
Tom Handcar: Tin and plastic. Tom pumps his vehicle as it travels with bump and go action and ringing bell.
66D.
Jerry Handcar: Same action as the Tom Handcar.

This group of plastic toys made in the late 70's or early 80's, although not yet collectible, is interesting, and will almost certainly be collected in the near future.

67A.
Tweety and Sylvester Alarm Clock: This wonderful toy has Sylvester chasing Tweety Bird around in a circle as Tweety calls out to you for help. Made in Taiwan.
67B.
Snoopy Doghouse: Woodstock acts as the controller for this radio control rolling doghouse. Made in Hong Kong.
67C.
Pluto: Remote control Pluto does just about what you would expect him to do. He runs around, barks, etc. Made in Hong Kong.

67D.
Spiderman Car: Spiderman turns his head as he actually steers this bump and go auto. Made in Hong Kong.
67E.
Drumming Pink Panther: Pink Panther with moving head beats on his drums and cymbals. There is a vinyl-headed version (shown) and a plush-headed version. Made in Taiwan.

This is just a small sampling of the many comic toys available today.

78

68A.
Santa Claus: Cloth and tin toy with a vinyl face and lighted eyes. He turns his head, sways his body, and rings the bell.

68B.
Santa on the Globe: Tin, cloth, paper, and vinyl. One of the most beautiful of all the battery toys. Santa sits on top of a rotating globe that is studded with twinkling stars. As he slowly spins, he shakes his head, pulls at his sack of toys and plays a "Jingle Bells" rhythm with his bell.

68C.
Santa Claus: Same action as 68A except the star he holds lights up instead of his eyes.

69A.
Santa Claus: Cloth, tin and vinyl Santa has same action as 68A, but is a much larger toy.

69B.
Santa in Rocker: Cloth and vinyl Santa sits on a tin case next to an artificial Christmas tree. The lights on the tree blink on and off as Santa rings a bell and rocks in his chair. He should be holding a Christmas stocking in his left hand. (It is missing here.)

70A.
Happy Santa: Tin, cloth, and vinyl Santa with a moving head beats on his drum and cymbals. Comes in two versions: one with lighted eyes, one without.
70B.
Happy Santa: Tin, cloth, and celluloid remote control toy. Santa walks with a turning head, plays his drum with one hand while ringing a bell with the other. The star on his hat lights.
70C.
Santa Scooter: Tin, cloth, and plastic toy. Santa rides and steers a bump and go scooter with headlight and ringing bell.
70D.
Santa Handcar: Tin, cloth, and vinyl Santa rides a bump and go handcar with a pumping movement and ringing sound.

71A.
Snowman: Plush, tin, and plastic toy. While he's obviously not a Santa, I thought he fit in pretty well. While turning his head and shaking his broom, the snowman keeps a styrofoam snowball suspended above his head. He has lighted eyes and a plastic pipe in his mouth (it is missing here).
71B.
Skiing Santa: Cloth, vinyl, and tin remote control Santa Claus with moving arms and head rolls around on skiis and rings a bell.
71C.
Santa on Roof: Cloth and vinyl Santa on a tin house. Santa moves his head and holds presents in one hand while ringing a bell in the other. This is one of several versions of this toy.
71D.
Santa Claus: Tin, cloth, and vinyl. A rather Satanic looking Santa rings a bell, stands up, then sits down while moving arms and head.

MONSTERS
[and other strange creatures]

72A.
Haunted House: Predominantly tin with a little plastic. One of the nicest looking and most unusual of all battery toys. Push buttons on the side of the house control the following actions: jumping black cat, moving window shade, opening door (revealing a vampire), a silhouette of a ghost flying past a lighted window, a skeleton who pops out of the chimney, shaking roof, whistling wind, and a scary, growling howl.

73A.
Laffun Head: Made in Korea in the late 70's. Plastic and cloth toy. When you pull his bowtie, this bizarre character opens and closes his eyes, sticks his tongue in and out, spits water from his mouth, and laughs uncontrollably. Many different variations.

73B.
Tiger Plaque: Very realistic looking vinyl tiger head is mounted on a tin plaque. When you pull a string, his eyes light up, his mouth opens and closes, and he roars.

73C.
Holiday Lanterns: These tin and glass lanterns are two of the many different ones I have seen. The glass domes light up, and some blink on and off. There are also Santas, snowmen, devils, and witches. Some are celluloid and tin.

74A.
Creeping Crawling Hand: Rubber and tin. Frankenstein's hand (see box section) pulls itself along the ground by the use of its fingers. Very few of these very rare toys survived, because the rubber used for the skin hardened and/or disintegrated over the years.

74B.
Nutty Mad Car: Tin and vinyl "far out" hotrodding monster drives his car in a very eccentric manner.

74C.
Golden Bat: This tin, cloth, and vinyl toy was called the Skull Head Robot in the past, for obvious reasons. In fact, he's not a robot at all, but a Japanese Super Hero much like our Spiderman. He walks with swinging arms and a lighted head.

74D.
Knight in Armor: When you hit the shield of this tin suit of armor with one of the arrows provided, the face lights up and it swings a sword.

74E.
The ????????: If anyone knows what this is supposed to be, please drop me a line. It is made of tin, cloth and straw. When you pull its string, this combination of a shell-less turtle and a native voodoo doll opens and closes its mouth, making a squeaking sound and moves its head up and down. The eyes also light.

75A.
75B. **Whistling Tree:** Tin and vinyl tree rolls with bump and go action as arms swing up and down, mouth and eyes open and close, and a loud whistling sound is emitted. A fantastic toy, (although I would imagine there were a few pairs of wet undies when these were first shown to impressionable youngsters.)

76A. **Walking Frankenstein:** Tin and vinyl remote control monster walks, bends over, opens and closes and raises and lowers his arms.

76B. **Prehistoric Monster:** Vinyl Godzilla-like monster with a tin bottom moves with bump and go action. His eyes light and he roars.

76C. **Barragon:** Tin and vinyl remote control monster walks with moving arms, opens his mouth, growls, and breathes smoke. The eyes and mouth light up. Made for the Japanese market, this toy is based on a monster from one of their horror films.

76D. **Jiras:** Another in the series of Japanese monsters. Same action as the Barragon (above).

76E. **Godzilla:** Same action as the Barragon (above). He's obviously popular in the States as well.

77A. **Mod Monster:** Tin, cloth and vinyl toy. Frankenstein moves his arms up and down and sways as if walking. He growls and suddenly loses his pants (see last figure). When his pants fall down, his face blushes red.

77B. **Monsturn - Turn Signal Frankenstein:** Obviously patterned after the first and last figure. This is a marginal battery toy (it hooks up to your car battery). When attached and placed in the rear window of the car, the lights in its hands signal turns and stops.

77C. **Frankenstein:** An earlier version of the Mod Monster. Frankenstein wears more traditional dress instead of a Nehru jacket.

78A. Snappy the Dragon: Plush, tin and plastic dragon moves along with a swaying tail. Each of his nine body segments has a yellow plastic fin on top. These fins light on and off in sequence as he moves. He stops, opens his mouth and blows bubbles.

MECHANICAL BANKS

Mechanical banks were the first group of battery toys considered collectible by the vintage toy collectors. Years before figural battery toys were considered anything but children's playthings, a few bank collectors started buying them as modern mechanicals. Mr. F.H. Griffith, probably the most famous of all bank collectors, has been a fan of Japanese toys for years. He has every known battery operated bank as part of his collection. All banks featured in this chapter, and the information about them were kindly provided by Mr. Griffith, for which I would like to thank him very much.

79A. **Santa on Roof Bank:** Tin, cloth, and vinyl. When the coin is inserted, he rings his bell, shakes the presents, moves his head, and his eyes light.

79B. **Santa at the Desk Bank:** Tin, cloth, and vinyl toy. Deposit a coin in the large phone and dial Santa's number. His phone will ring, he'll pick it up, and nod his head as if speaking to you, all the time writing Merry Xmas on a lighted piece of paper.

80A. **Fishing Bears Bank:** All tin toy. Place a coin in the slot to start the action. Papa bear fishes in the pond and pulls up a fish. Mama moves a pan to accept the fish, Baby moves his arms up and down and Papa puts the fish into Baby's sand pail.

80B. **Cowboy Savings Bank:** All tin. When the coin is dropped into the slot, the horse gallops as the cowboy rocks in the saddle. Arms and hat move freely.

80C. **Globe Explorer Bank:** All tin. The coin is deposited automatically, and the ships make seven revolutions of the globe, always stopping over the USA.

81A. **Clown Vending Machine Bank:** Mostly tin. Place the coin in the slot, and the clown turns the crank, bending back and forth. The candy drops into the chute.

81B. **Organ Grinder Bank:** Tin, cloth, and vinyl. The organ grinder turns the crank of the organ when the coin is deposited, while music plays and the monkey bounces and turns on top.

81C. **Gypsy Witch Fortune Teller Bank:** Cloth and vinyl figure on tin base. Place a coin in the slot and her head nods, the hand with the ball moves back and forth, and the right hand is raised. Her eyes flash three times, the hand lowers, and a fortune card shoots out from under her sleeve.

82A. **Red Cab Bank:** Tin taxi made in China. Deposit the coin and the cab rolls. A recent toy.

82B. **Yellow Cab Bank:** Same action as Red Cab. Much earlier Japanese version.

82C.

82D. **Pepsi and Coke Vending Machine Banks:** When the coin is deposited, these banks vend real soda into a glass. Tin and plastic.

83A.
The Hand From Uncle Bank: When the coin is placed on the spot provided, a hand comes out and scoops it into the bank. Plastic.

83B.
Eightball Bank: Plastic and tin bank. When a coin is deposited, a clown shows behind the number eight.

83C.
Down the Drain Bank: Plastic and tin. The coin is placed in the slot, the toilet lid opens, and a man holding a "Help" sign pops out.

83D.
Clown Bank: Plastic. When coin is placed in his hand, the clown's eyes blink on and off, and he flips the coin into his mouth.

83E.
Bartender Bank: Tin and plastic. A coin is placed on the spot provided. It shoots into the cash register which rings. The drinker raises his mug.

84A. **Uncle Sam High Taxes Bank:** Mostly plastic. A coin is placed on the coin spot. The figure moves as though kicking the coin into Uncle Sam's hat.

84B. **Hole in One Bank:** Mostly plastic. The coin is placed on the coin spot, the golfer swings his club, the coin goes into the 18th hole and the flag moves.

84C.
84D. **Bowling Bank:** Mostly plastic. In both examples, the coin is placed on the coin spot, and the bowler shoots the coin towards the pins. In 84C, the pins move as though knocked down. A light flashes.

93

85A. **Luncheonette Bank:** Tin and plastic. When the coin is inserted, the girl moves over to pour a cup of coffee.

85B. **Treasure Chest Bank:** Plastic and cloth. When you deposit the coin, the girl pulls down her towel, exposing her lighted breasts. She then pulls the towel up with her other hand, revealing the message "More Money Please" written on her leg.

85C. **Gofer Bank - Robotron:** Plastic and rubber. Made in Hong Kong. He jiggles when a full glass is placed on his tray, and moves forward with a rasping noise. A coin placed in the slot on his head stops the noise and the jiggling. After you drink and put the empty glass on the tray, he goes away.

86A. **Haunted House Bank:** Plastic, made in Hong Kong. A hand comes out of a window, and removes the coin from the chimney, as the inside of the building lights and a shadow figure dances inside.

86B. **Haunted House Bank:** Tin and plastic, made in USA. When the coin is placed on the front porch, the door lights up, and a ghost comes out of the door to get it. This bank was at one time sold at the Haunted Mansion gift shop in Disney World and Disneyland.

86C. **Tweety and Sylvester Bank:** Plastic, made in Hong Kong. When a coin is inserted in this late 70's bank, Sylvester tries to catch Tweety, and Tweety's voice calls out for help.

86D. **Buddy L Mickey Mouse Disco Bank:** Plastic, made in Hong Kong. When the coin is deposited, Mickey's arm moves, the record turns, and music plays.

ROBOTS
AND ASTRONAUTS

Once again I would like to thank Mr. F.H. Griffith for giving me access to his collection. Without his help, this chapter would have been extremely difficult. Most of the robots and astronauts pictured here are from his collection. Nowhere else are there so many rare robots in such excellent condition. Unfortunately, for each toy I photographed, there were probably three or four that I left out. This could not be avoided, but I did try to include most of the rare and impressive pieces.

Robots really belong in a class by themselves. In recent years, they have become the most popular battery operated toy, being collected by robot collectors as well as battery toy collectors, and have increased in value immensely.

As years go by and domestic robots become more a reality than science fiction, the early ideas of what robots would look and act like (attacking, fighting monsters with shooting guns) will become more and more amusing. This nostalgia factor added to their striking appearance and intricate actions should keep robots among the most popular toys for collectors.

87A.
Electric Robot and Son: Mostly plastic, made in USA. Very early robot rolls forward and backwards with lighted eyes and turning head. A buzzer can be operated by a button on his back to send Morse Code messages. A drawer in his chest holds two small tools. There is a red and black variation. This robot was sold without the son as the Electric Robot.

87B. **Answer Game:** Mostly tin. This robot is a working adding machine. He adds and subtracts, his eyes blink, and a disc revolves in his head.

88A.
Mechanized Robot - Robby Space Patrol: Tin with some plastic. This toy is based on the Robbie the Robot character in the movie *Forbidden Planet*. It moves with bump and go and mystery action. Red and green lights blink when the robot hits something.

89A.
89B.
Robbie the Robot: Tin with a plastic head dome. He walks with moving pistons in his head and rotating antennas on his ears. The silver version on left is very rare.
89C.
Planet Robot: Tin with rubber hands. Remote control version of the black wind-up Planet Robot. He walks as his head and chest light.
89D.
Space Trooper: Tin and plastic remote control Robbie rolls forward or backwards with a stepping motion.

Inside his head, radar spins and a red light goes on. Also comes in black.
89E.
Robbie: Tin, plastic and rubber remote control robot walks with moving lighted pistons in his head. There is also a silver variation.

Like 88A, these are all based on the Robbie the Robot from the great science fiction movie **Forbidden Planet**.

90A.
Man in Space: Tin and celluloid. An extremely unusual tin astronaut with a propeller on his back actually flies and can be manuvered. The tin remote control is beautifully lithographed, and the box has great litho inside and out.

90B.
Robot: Mostly tin remote control robot walks with moving arms and blows baby powder from his mouth. Both his eyes and the lantern in his right hand light.

91A. **Colonel Hap Hazard:** Tin and plastic astronaut walks with swinging arms and a spinning lighted antenna on his helmet.

91B. **High Bounce Moon Scout:** Tin and plastic remote control astronaut with the same action as the above figure, except a small door also opens in his chest, and he shoots out high bouncing "super balls".

91C. **Earthman:** Mostly tin remote control astronaut walks forward, and lifts and fires his space gun.

91D. **Spaceman:** Mostly tin astronaut walks with stepping motion (one side at a time moves forward). He has swinging arms and a lighted helmet.

91E. **Astronaut:** Mostly tin. Walks with moving arms, one hand holding a ray gun, the other a lantern. Lantern and helmet light up. Nice litho on his remote control box.

92A.
92B.
92C. **Astronaut:** Three color variations of a very nice tin toy. The spaceman walks forward as an antenna spins over his head. He stops, lifts his gun up with both hands, and shoots with flashing light and sound. The green version 92B is the hardest to find.

92D. **Remote Control Astronaut:** Mostly tin astronaut holding gun. Walks with swinging arms and a lighted helmet.

92E. **Spaceman:** A remote control version of 91D.

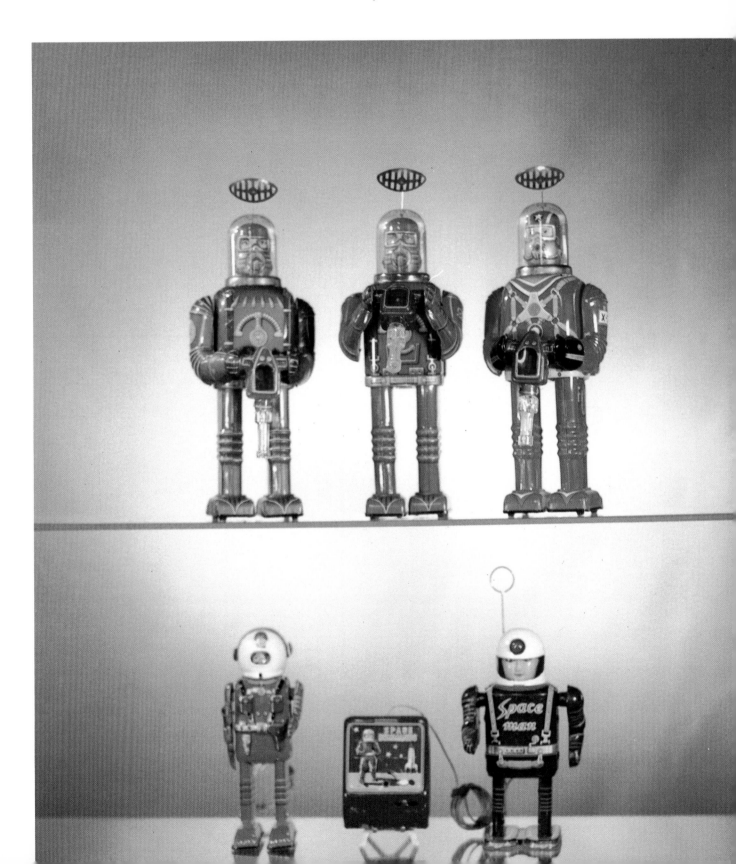

93A. **Cragstan Astronaut:** Tin and plastic spaceman walks, stops and moves his gun up and down as he fires it with flashing light and shooting sound. The battery case on his back is shaped like oxygen tanks.

93B. **Great Astronaut:** Tin and plastic astronaut is switched on when his antenna is pushed into his helmet. He walks with swinging arms and a rotating color bar around his neck. The TV screen on his chest lights up to show moving pictures of outer space. Also comes in a grey robot version, called "Television Spaceman".

93C. **Astronaut:** A non-Cragstan version of 93A. Same action.

94A. **Missile M Robot:** Tin and plastic. The radar antenna is inserted to start the action. He walks with swinging arms, and his eyes light. Large red rockets shoot out of his chest and go back in.

94B. **Moon Explorer:** Tin and plastic. Put the antenna in to start the action. He walks, his eyes light, his arms swing, the clock hands revolve, and colored wheels revolve in two windows on either side of the clock. A piston-lever operates in a lower window.

94C. **Rocket Man:** Tin and plastic. Very similar in appearance and actions to 94B, except this one has rockets that fire automatically peeking over his head. The robot's head lifts back, revealing a tin astronaut.

95A.
Train Robot: Tin with some plastic details. A toggle switch in front starts the bump and go action. His arms swing, eyes light alternately, his ears light, and he makes a loud whistling "whoo whoo" like a train.

95B.
Target Robot: Tin robot comes with a black tin gun that shoots rubber tipped darts. When activated, he moves forward, arms swinging. When you fire the dart and hit him, he makes a screaming noise, turns, and retreats. The eyes light, the mouth shows a "lightening" effect, and he turns and comes at you again.

96A.
Lavender Robot: Tin robot with bump and go action, swinging arms, and lighted eyes and ears.
96B.
Radicon Robot: Tin and plastic radio controlled robot. (Probably the first radio controlled robot.) The robot moves with swinging arms and lighted eyes. A button on the remote control triggers a spark and light in the chest, and eccentric action (robot stops, turns, backs up, etc.).

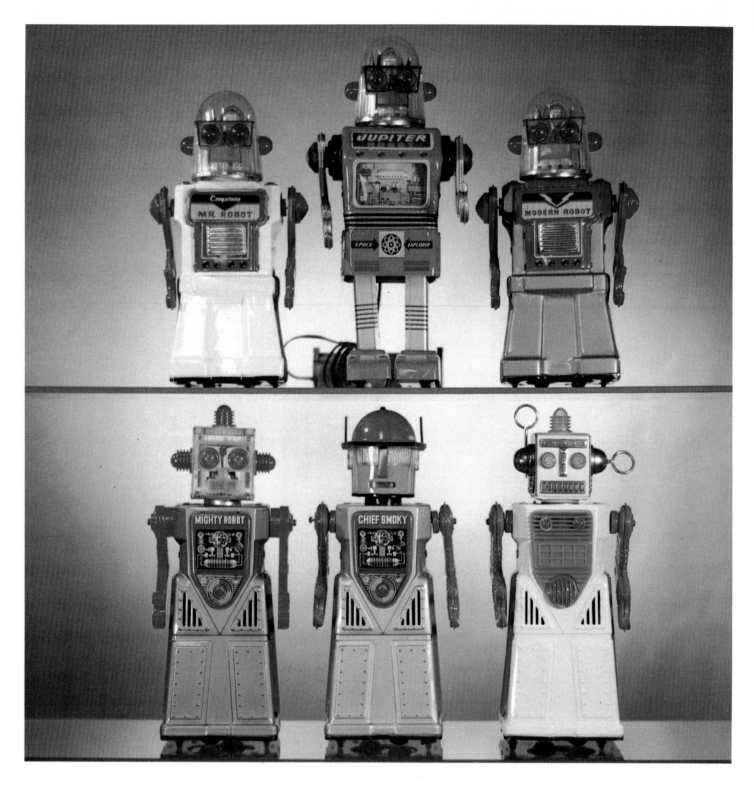

97A.
Mr. Robot: Tin and plastic robot with bump and go action, swinging arms, and a complex contraption in his head that lights up and spins around.
97B.
Jupiter Robot: Very rare tin remote control walking version of Mr. Robot.
97C.
Modern Robert: Another variation of Mr. Robot.
97D.
Mighty Robot: Tin and plastic. The robot has bump and go action, and swinging arms. His head lights up, and sixteen gears spin inside it.

97E.
Chief Smoky: Tin and plastic. Bump and go action, arms swing, head lights, and smoke blows from the top.
97F.
Chief Robot Man: Tin and plastic. The head lights up and turns, and the antennas spin as he moves with bump and go action. This is one of several color variations.

98A.
98B.
98C.
Zoomer: A tin robot holding a wrench walks with lighted eyes. These are three of at least five different variations.
98D.
Radar Robot: All tin remote control robot walks with lighted eyes and a light in his radar antenna.
98E.
Musical Drummer Robot: Mostly tin remote control robot walks and beats on a drum. With lighted eyes.

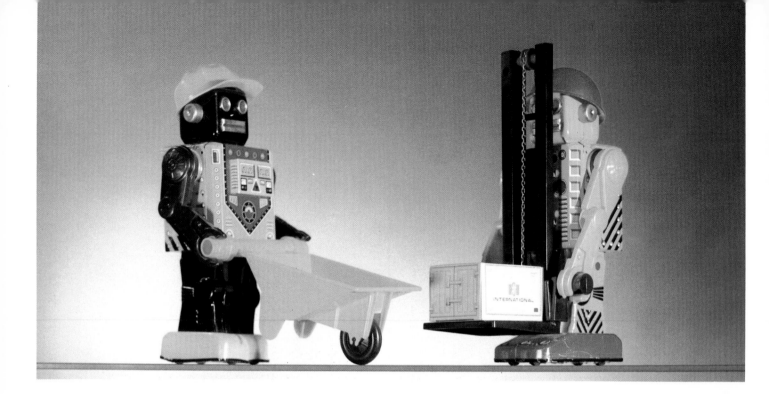

99A.
Busy Cart Robot: Tin and plastic robot walks, stops, lifts up and empties a wheelbarrow.
99B.
Forklift Robot: Tin and plastic robot walks and operates a forklift device. Comes with a cardboard box.

99C.
Original Lost in Space Robot: Plastic, made in USA. Rolls straight ahead or turns to either side. Has blinking light and movable arms. From the TV show.
99D.
Lost in Space Robot: Later, plastic version of 98C. Made in Hong Kong. Walks with a swiveling action, stops with blinking lights and space sound.

100A.
Gigantor: Tin and plastic remote control robot walks, turns and shoots his fists like rockets. See Gigantor on following page.
100B.
Robot Control: Tin robot walks forward or backward by remote control. His eyes blink, and his arms swing.
100C.
Golden Roto Robot: Tin and plastic robot opens at the shoulders to insert batteries. He walks as the top half of his body slowly revolves 360 degrees. Guns fire from his chest. Also comes in a grey version.

100D.
Talking Robot: Mostly tin robot rolls on a friction motor. Push the button on his stomach and he says four different things in a macho voice.
100E.
Mike Robot: An early plastic robot. When you speak into an attached microphone, the sound comes out of the robot's chest as his mouth opens and his eyes blink in time with your voice. When you pull him, he rolls with a clicking sound.
100F.
Piston Head Robot: Early 70's plastic and tin robot. He walks, and has moving lighted pistons in his head.

101A.
Moonlight Man: Tin figure with vinyl head and cape walks with swinging arms.

This is one of a large series of Japanese astronauts, robots and assorted Super Heros. Made in both windup and battery versions.
101B.
Mat Astronaut: Similar to Moonlight Man.
101C.
Millerman: Similar to Moonlight Man.

101D.
Astronaut: Strange variation of the Cragstan Astronaut, 93A with a vinyl boy's face replacing the tin astronaut head.
101E.
Gigantor: Tin, plastic, and rubber robot walks with swinging arms and lighted eyes. He was a TV cartoon character here in the United States in the mid 60's. In Japan, he is known as Iron Man #28.

102A.
Smoking Spaceman: Mostly tin robot walks with moving arms and a rotating lighted color dome in his head. He stops, his eyes blink, and he blows smoke from his mouth. He also comes in a grey version.
102B.
Wheel-A-Gear Robot: Tin and plastic. He walks with swinging arms, shifting eyes and spinning wheels and gears in his lighted chest. There is another version of this robot called Blink-A-Gear that has lighted blinking eyes and only gears in the chest.
102C.
Rosko Astronaut: Tin and plastic spaceman walks, lifts his lighting walkie talkie to his head, and sends a message in the form of a beeping sound. There is also a red variation.

111

103A.

103B. **Mr. Mercury:** Mostly tin robot walks, bends over, opens and closes his arms, and raises and lowers his arms. Remote control. The second version shown has plastic arms and his chest lights.

103C. **Space Explorer:** Mostly tin toy looks like a TV set when closed up. By pushing the button on his head, you start his action: Head, arms, and legs extend from his body, and a picture appears on the TV screen on his chest. He steps forward with his eyes blinking, stops, and folds back into a box and turns off. There are at least two other variations. One is red, and the other is black. They both have a normal on/off switch on their backs.

103D. **Mr. Atomic:** Tin and plastic robot moves with bump and go action. His feet move up and down, the arms swing loosely, and the face panel lights in various patterns and colors. He whistles or beeps, depending on his color. Also made in blue variation.

104A. **Robotank Z:** Tin and plastic robot rolls with bump and go action. Arms on the side move the controls back and forth as he goes. The guns in front shoot.

104B. **Space Commander:** Tin astronaut with tin litho treads instead of legs. Moves with bump and go action as chest doors open and shooting guns emerge.

104C. **Thunder Robot:** Tin and plastic. Has spinning antenna and spinning light in head. He walks, stops, raises his arms, and guns hidden in the palms of his hands flash and shoot.

104D. **Dino:** Tin and plastic robot walks, stops, his head splits in half, and a red creature's head appears. The head lights and the creature's mouth opens and closes as he growls.

105A.
105B.
Directional Robot: Mostly tin robot moves with bump and go action. His head turns as he looks in each direction that he moves. Shown in the two color variations.
105C.
Radar Robot: Tin and plastic robot walks as his chest lights, and his gears spin.

105D.
Robot: Tin and plastic. Walks forward with swinging arms. Has moving color bands in mouth. Shapes inside head spin, and the whole head revolves.
105E.
Robot 8: Mostly tin robot walks. Has a psychedelic kaleidoscope action in the circle on the chest.

106A.
Mini Robotank: Tin and plastic robot with bump and go action and shooting gun. His arms hold and move the levers on his sides.

106B.
Walking Robot: Tin remote control robot with a plastic dome over his head. He steps forward with swinging arms. There is also a variation without a dome.

106C.
Mini Robotank TR2: Same action as first Mini Robotank.

106D.
Powder Robot: Primitive looking remote control robot. Powder is placed in his head and he blows it out of his mouth with a popping sound. Eyes light and arms move as he walks.

106E.
Robot: Tin remote control robot walks forward or backward. The eyes light and arms move.

106F.
Mr. Robot Mechanical Brain: All tin robot walks powered by a wind-up motor. A battery placed in his head operates alternately blinking lights in the ends of his arms.

107A.
Engine Robot: Tin and plastic robot walks with swinging arms, rotating gears in chest and engine sound. Eyes, ears, and dome light up. There are numerous variations available.

107B.
Robot: Tin and plastic. Rolls forward, stops, and the chest doors open, exposing shooting guns. The visor opens, revealing an astronaut's face inside. There is also a silver variation.

107C.
Space Scout: Mostly tin. Astronaut walks with moving arms, door opens and a lighted, shooting gun comes out. There is also a robot version and a silver astronaut version.

107D.
Gear Robot: Mostly tin robot walks with swinging arms, moving gears in the chest, and three lights that blink on and off in sequence. He has a switch on his head which operates him at fast or slow speed.

107E.
Mr. Patrol: Mostly tin robot walks as dials move up and down in chest. He stops, arms raise up, and a loud siren goes off. Also comes in a robot version.

107F.
Turn Signal Robot: Mostly tin. Walks with moving arms and antenna, eight spinning gears in his chest, alternately blinking red and green arrow lights, and a head dome with revolving red/green light.

108A.
Robot Commando: Plastic remote control robot, made in USA. He rolls, turns, throws balls from his hands, shoots rockets from under his hat and his eyes roll, all at your command. One of a very few battery toys (of that time) advertised heavily on TV.

108B.
Pepo: Tin and plastic radio controlled robot (vintage unknown). He rolls and changes direction. With flashing lights and space sound. Made in Spain.

109A. **Hysterical Harry:** Plastic robot with bump and go action rolls with shaking arms. He stops, his head moves up and down, and his mouth opens, revealing lighted teeth as he laughs hysterically.

109B. **Giant Robot:** Mostly plastic remote control robot rolls with moving arms and legs and lighting eyes.

109C. **Mr. Lem** [**Lunar Excursion Man**]: Plastic robot walks with swinging arms and whirring sound. Made in Hong Kong.

109D. **Gear Robot:** Made in Hong Kong. Plastic robot walks, arms swing and gears spin.

109E. **Krome Dome:** Plastic and tin robot with bump and go action. When he stops, he actually grows taller and his arms extend out, his mouth opens and he lets out a screeching sound. Eyes also light.

109F. **Lunar Spaceman:** Plastic robot-like astronaut walks, doors open, and shooting guns appear. Made in Hong Kong.

110A. **Dalek:** Plastic robot from the British TV show *Dr. Who.* Has bump and go action with flashing light. Many variations in color (red, grey, silver, and black), size and action. Made from the 60's through the 70's, in England.

110B. **Tiny Robot:** Plastic and metal. This great robot walks with swinging arms and a see-thru body showing his working mechanism. Very quiet when in operation.

110C. **Talking Dalek:** All plastic, made in Hong Kong (70's). This version of 110A says approximately ten different phrases. There is also a variation which features *Dr. Who's* talking robot dog, K-9.

110D. **Explo:** Plastic robot walks and literally falls to pieces. Made in Hong Kong.

110E. **Mr. Brain:** Plastic and paper learning tool for children. He buzzes, and his red and green eyes light to signal right or wrong answers to his questions. Made in USA.

110F. **Jupiter Robot:** Mostly plastic remote control Robbie-like robot walks with spinning gears in his chest.

111A.
Missile Robot: Plastic and tin robot walks and stops with rotating body. Has four missiles on his head to aim and fire.
111B.
Mr. Monster: Plastic, made in Hong Kong. Walks with eight spider-like legs, and climbs over obstacles with spinning antenna, moving arms, blinking lights and space sound.
111C.
Mr. Mercury: Plastic and tin robot walks with flashing lights.

111D.
Space Explorer: Tin and plastic spaceman walks, stops as door drops down to reveal a screen with lighted, moving space scene.
111E.
Attacking Martian: Plastic and tin robot walks and stops with guns firing from chest.
111F.
Swivel-O-Matic Astronaut: Tin and plastic astronaut walks as body rotates and guns shoot.

MISCELLANEOUS VEHICLES

In most of the other chapters of this book I've tried to be as complete as possible. Of course, there are many animal toys and robots that are not included here, but I've photographed most of the more desirable toys and, a large variety of the others. This was not possible in this chapter. There are probably as many vehicular toys as all other battery toys put together. Therefore, I've taken a different approach to the vehicle toys. Instead of describing individual toys in detail, I will discuss the different categories to which these toys belong (ships, buses, space toys, motorcycles, etc.). In this way, I can cover a topic that would otherwise require an entire volume of its own.

There are quite a few bus collectors out there, and quite a few battery-operated buses for them to collect. Some of the earlier ones (such as the Sightseeing Bus) are very nicely detailed with great actions. These are obviously more valuable than plain looking buses that just roll (such as the City Line Bus).

112A.
City Line Bus: Tin bus with bump and go action.
112B.
Stop and Go School Bus: Stop and go action with flashing lights.

112C.
Sound Bus: Moves with sounding horn.
112D.
Sightseeing Bus: A man sticks his head out of the window as bus rolls.

Motorcycles have been a popular collectible toy for a number of years, although the most desired ones are wind-ups. Of the relatively few tin, battery-operated motorcycles, the two pictured are probably the best.

Unlike motorcycles, there are a large number of battery-operated planes. The prop planes are more desirable than the jets, and you should look for examples patterned after actual aircraft.

Through the years, little boys have looked up to policemen and firemen, and there is no better way to cash in on this than to make a large variety of police and fire chief cars. The most popular versions feature passengers who are animated (steering, shooting a gun, speaking on the phone, etc.).

113A. **Motorcycle:** A man actually gets off and on his motorcycle. Stop and go action with working headlight.

113B. **Police Motorcycle:** Same action as first motorcycle.

113C. **Mystery Jet Plane:** Pilot steers bump and go action fighter plane.

113D. **Highway Patrol:** Policeman drives car with siren sound.

Here's an assortment of various vehicles that don't belong in any specific category. All have very nice actions and are well-made.

114A.
114B. **Television Trucks:** These tin bus-like vehicles have moving cameramen mounted on top. TV screens on the vehicles light up and show pictures.

114C. **Railroad Handcar:** The tin men pump up and down as the handcar travels on a rubber track.

114D. **Forklift Truck:** The driver operates the controls of this tin vehicle.

115A.
Merry-Go-Round Truck: This beautifully made tin toy is very popular with carnival toy collectors. The truck rolls forward with ringing sound as the carousel spins. Also made in a ferris wheel version. There's a nice series of smaller, friction powered carnival trucks that includes a version of the merry-go-round truck featured here.

115B.
Silver Streak: These train engines are one of the few tin toys still found in the stores today. Of the countless examples available, almost all have the same actions (bump and go, whistle sound, etc.), and very few of them are desired by collectors.

115C.
115D.
115E.
Farm and construction machinery, tractors, bulldozers, and plows comprise this group of vehicles. While there are collectors for these toys, they are not as valuable as their robot-driven versions.

116A.
Fire engines have made fine gifts for children for the past century. The battery-operated versions, while still popular with children, have not yet become overly desirable to collectors. There are some very well-made fire engines that are easy to sell, but the common, simple versions (such as the one pictured here) are not in that category.

116B.
There are trucks of every size and description available to collectors: delivery trucks, construction trucks, and many others. Probably the most wanted are those that advertise actual products, such as the Coca Cola truck pictured.

Tanks, jeeps, helicopters, and any other military vehicle that has existed in real life, has at one time or another also existed as a toy. The actions of these battery toys tend to mirror those of their real counterparts.

116C.
Jeep: One soldier drives while the other operates the gun.

116D.
Combat Tank: Rolls with spinning turret and shooting gun.

The category "ships and boats" includes the one-man speedboat, ocean liners and everything in between. While a few purists will only collect toys that will actually work in the water, some of the nicest battery operated boats were made to roll on dry land.

117A.
Ocean Liner: Very impressive ship rolls with flashing lights and spinning radar.

117B.
Aircraft Carrier: Moves forward as planes on the side go up and down in elevators, the helicopter takes off, signal lights flash, radar revolves, and planes on the deck taxi and take off. Rockets fire manually.

117C.
Thunder Jet: Remote control speedboat works in water.

117D.
Nautilus Submarine: Subs have become increasingly popular over the last few years, and the Nautilus is one of the more famous ones. Runs in water with flashing lights.
117E.
Captain Kidd Pirate Ship: Another land-going vessel with bump and go action. This toy also shoots caps, a very unusual action for a battery toy.

Space travel has been a subject often explored by movies and TV over the past thirty years. Toy makers cashed in on this extraterrestrial preoccupation by producing countless space related toys. Some people only collect the toys patterned after actual spacecraft (Lunar Module, Apollo and Mercury capsules, Sputnik, etc.). Others prefer the fantasy space toys (flying saucers, space tanks, etc.). Whichever you prefer, most space toys have ingenious actions, and they make a fine collection.

118A.
Mars Rocket Ship: A fantasy spaceship.
118B.
Space Captain: Apollo capsule docks with Lunar Module.
118C.
Cape Canaveral Truck: Monitors satellites.

118D.
Space Survey Saucer: One of many nice flying saucers.
118E.
Space Patrol Tank: Nicely detailed multi-action tank.

It's a debatable point whether these toys belong with robots or with vehicles. I've always considered them robots but they are generally not as popular as their figural cousins. In any case, here are just a few of the numerous robot-driven vehicles available.

119A.
Piston Tractor: Mostly tin, rolls with moving pistons and fan belt.
119B.
Radar Tractor: Mostly tin, rolls with bump and go action and lighted radar.
119C.
Robot Tractor: Mostly tin. Rolls, engine parts move, robot's head lights.

119D.
Space Robot Car: Mostly tin car with bump and go action, blows balls in the air.
119E.
Robot Bulldozer: Mostly tin. The robot's eyes light, blade of bulldozer moves.
119F.
Robot Car X-9: Mostly tin. Robot steers bump and go car as marbles bounce around.

CARS

Collecting scale model cars is not restricted to battery toys. In fact, there are far more Japanese cars made with friction motors. But, whether friction, battery, or wind-up, there are certain things looked for by most car collectors.

Probably the most important is authentic detail. Cadillac collectors don't want to buy a car with a Cadillac body, a Chevy grill, and Buick headlights. Cadillac collectors want a toy that is as close in detail to the actual car as possible. The same can be said of any collector who is collecting a specific make of car.

Size is another factor to keep in mind. Generally, the smaller toys (under eight inches) were cheaper, and therefore lacked the workmanship that ten to twelve inch models had.

Some collectors collect only one specific car. There are collectors of VWs, Edsels, Corvettes, Jaguars, Mustangs, and probably every other car made. However, some makes are much more desirable than others. Obviously, there are more Cadillac collectors than Plymouth Valiant collectors. Usually, the most distinctive cars in real life make the most desirable toys.

I would like to thank Mr. Dale Kelley, publisher of *Antique Toy World* magazine, for providing the photographs and information used in this chapter.

120A.
1960's Plymouth TV Wagon: Manufactured by Ichiko. Mostly tin car rolls with working lights. Camera lights and turns.

120B.
1950's Plymouth: Manufactured by Alps. Tin car rolls forward and reverse.

121A.
1950's Cadillac: Manufactured by Marusan. Tin car rolls forward with working lights.

121B.
1950's Cadillac Convertible: Manufactured by T.N. Tin auto moves forward.

121C.
1960's Cadillac: Manufactured by Bandai. Mostly tin car goes forward and reverse. Has working headlights, horn, and gear shift.

122.
1950's Buick: Tin friction car with battery powered
lights. Manufactured by Marusan. Two color variations
plus the box are shown.

123A.
1950's Thunderbird Convertible: Manufactured by T.N.
Tin car rolls forward with working lights.

123B.
1950's Thunderbird Convertible: Manufactured by T.N.
Tin car with composition driver rolls forward.

123C.
1950's Thunderbird: Tin remote control car rolls
forward. Has retracting roof.

124A.
1960's Corvette: Manufactured by Ichida. Tin car rolls with opening headlights, stop and go action, and horn sound.

124B.
1960's Corvette: Manufactured by Taiyo. Rolls, with working lights and non-fall action.

124C.
1960's Corvette: A color variation of 124B.

125A.
1960's Mustang: Manufactured by Bandai. Tin car rolls, has opening door.

125B.
1960's Mustang: Manufactured by Bandai. Tin car rolls forward and has skidding action.

125C.
1960's Mustang: Manufacturer unknown. Tin car rolls forward with non-fall action.

126A.
1950's Benz: Manufactured by T.N. Tin car rolls forward.

126B.
Box: For 126A.

126C.
Benz Racer: Manufactured by Marusan. Tin car rolls with lights. Stop and go action.

127A. **1960's 220 S Benz:** Manufactured by S.S.S. Tin car rolls forward, has working lights and opening trunk.

127B. **1960's Benz:** Manufactured by Ichiko. Tin car rolls forward, radio antenna moves up and down.

127C. **1960's Benz Taxi:** Manufactured by Bandai. Tin taxi moves with bump and go action and working lights. As it stops, the door opens and closes.

128A. **1960's Volkswagon:** Manufactured by Taiyo. Tin car rolls with non-fall action.

128B. **1960's Volkswagon:** Manufactured by Bandai. Tin car with sun roof rolls with visible working engine.

128C. **1960's Volkswagon Convertible:** Manufactured by TM. Tin car rolls forward.

128D.
1960's Volkswagon Convertible: Manufactured by T.N. Mostly tin car rolls forward. Has working headlights and horn.

129A. **Volkswagon Convertible:** Manufactured by Bandai. Mostly tin remote control car goes forward and in reverse, and steers.

129B. **1960's Volkswagon:** Manufactured by Bandai. Rolls with visible working engine.

129C. **1960's Volkswagon Microbus:** Manufactured by Bandai. Tin car rolls forward.

129D.**1960's Volkswagon Pick-up:** Manufactured by Bandai. Remote control tin truck rolls forward and in reverse and steers.

130A. **1960's Porsche:** Manufactured by Bandai. Tin car rolls forward, has opening doors.

130B. **1960's Porsche:** Manufactured by Daiya. Tin car rolls forward.

130C. **1960's Jaguar:** Manufactured by Bandai. Tin car rolls forward, hood opens to reveal lighted engine.

131A. **1960's Rolls Royce:** Manufactured by Bandai. Tin car rolls forward with working lights.

131B. **1960's Ferrari:** Manufactured by Bandai. Tin car rolls forward and in reverse, with working lights, horn, and a working gear shift.

131C. **1960's Citroen:** Manufactured by Bandai. Tin car moves forward with working lights.

132A. **1950's Opel:** Manufactured by Yonezawa. Tin car rolls with working lights.

132B. **1950's Lincoln:** Manufactured by Yonezawa. Remote control tin car goes forward and in reverse.

132C. **1950's Mercury:** Manufactured by L.H.C. Tin car rolls forward.

133A. **1960's Camero:** Manufactured by Taiyo. Tin car rolls forward, has working lights and non-fall action.

133B. **1960's Pontiac Firebird:** Manufactured by Bandai. Tin car moves forward, and has working wipers.

133C. **1960's Cougar:** Manufactured by Taiyo. Tin car moves forward with non-fall action.

134A. **1960's Ford:** Tin car rolls forward, and has retracting roof.

134B. **1960's Ford GT:** Manufactured by Bandai. Tin auto rolls with bump and go action; stops; and hood and trunk open, revealing a lighted engine.

134C. **1960's Toronado:** Manufacturer unknown. Tin car moves forward with opening headlights.

135A. **1960's Corvair:** Manufactured by Bandai. Mostly tin car rolls with opening hood.

135B. **1960's Sea Hawk:** Manufactured by Yonezawa. Tin and plastic car rolls forward.

135C. **1960's Ford Gyron:** Manufactured by Ichida. Tin car moves forward. Has opening top. Also comes in a red and black remote control version.

MINI WIND-UP VERSIONS OF BATTERY TOYS

Technically, this chapter does not belong in this book. However, in the last few years a number of battery toy collectors have started buying these toys for their collections. They are simply small wind-up or friction toys with the same appearance and action as specific battery toys. They have similar actions to their big brothers, although sometimes less complex. Their clothing and other features vary from being somewhat similar to being almost an exact copy of the battery toy. All in all, they make a very interesting collection.

In the descriptions, the number in parentheses indicates the number of the photo where the battery toy is shown and described.

136A. **Frankenstein:** One of the nicest of all battery toys (76A) towers above his younger brother. The wind-up came in at least two variations, one mostly tin, the other (pictured here) is mostly plastic.

137A.
Great Garloo: This was my favorite toy when I was a child. He is a mostly plastic remote control monster who rolls, steers, bends over, and opens and closes his hands. He is holding the miniature wind-up version of himself. (Son of Garloo) Like the Frankenstein, the wind-up comes in mostly tin or mostly plastic versions.
137B.
Secret Agent Spy Car: This is the non-remote control battery operated car discussed earlier (60A). In front of it is a friction version with similar actions.

Here are the Japanese Super Heros discussed earlier (101A thru C). There are at least ten different battery operated characters available, and more than thirty of the wind-ups. All are tin with vinyl heads. They walk and swing their arms.

138A.
Millerman: Battery and wind-up version.
138B.
Ultraman Leo: Battery version (wind-up not shown).
138C.
Mat Astronaut: Battery and wind-up astronaut.
138D.
Moonlight Man: The battery version is shown (wind-up not shown).

139A. **Strutting Sam:** Wind-up and battery version of Strutting Sam (50B). The wind-up also comes in a white man variation.

139B. **Dancing Couple:** Battery version (49E) and wind-up Dancing Couple. The wind-up is tin with vinyl heads. It has the same action as the battery toy, minus the music.

139C. **Piggy Chef:** Three sizes of the Piggy Chef are shown. On the far right is the battery toy (11D). In the center is a wind-up variation who is cooking spaghetti, and finally, on the left is the miniature of the miniature, a stoveless pig who flips a ham and egg omlette.

140A. **Knitting Cat:** Wind-up and battery-operated (15C).

140B. **Monkey Artist:** Battery-operated and wind-up (15D).

140C. **Shoeshine Monkey:** Wind-up and battery-operated (23B).

140D. **Shoemaker Bear:** Battery-operated and wind-up (23A).

141A. **Caterpillars:** Plush and tin, crawl with similar action. The battery version (7A) has lighted eyes, which the wind-up lacks.

141B. **Bengali Tiger:** Wind-up and battery operated (5D). The Marx toy company seemed to transform quite a few of their popular battery toys into wind-ups. Usually, these wind-ups were faithful to the battery-operated toy in both appearance and action. These tigers are a good example.

142A. **Nutty Mad Indian:** Another Marx creation, the wind-up has the same charm (or lack of it) as the larger battery toy (45A).

142B. **Bartender:** This wind-up pours and drinks with smacking lips, but can't match the battery toy (48A) when it comes to the lighting face, smoking ears or swaying motion.

142C. **Fred Riding Dino:** A marginal miniature version of his larger alter ego (59C). It is made of tin instead of cloth; the action is much simpler; and it seems only Dino is in miniature (if anything, Fred has grown). Still, I guess in spirit he belongs in this chapter. The wind-up also came with Barney Rubble riding Dino.

143A.
Pinkee the Farmer Truck: Friction and battery operated 42A. The friction version is minus the moving pistons.

143B.
Dog Pianist: Battery version (13B) on left and wind-up version have the same action. The pianos are the same size, only the dog is smaller.

143C.
Trumpet Monkey: The battery operated (30B) and the wind-up monkey are only vaguely similar. The wind-up monkey is standing instead of sitting, and has no bee buzzing near his ear. He is however, playing the same type of horn.

144A.
Dolly Seamstress: Wind-up and battery operated (46B).
144B.
Miss Friday Typist: Wind-up and battery operated (46D).
144C.
Drinking Panda Bear: Battery and wind-up (21F).
144D.
Drinking Monkey: Battery and wind-up (21E).

The wind-up Drinking Panda Bear and Monkey do not actually pour liquid as the battery operated versions do, nor do their eyes light.

153

Here are two more of the Marx miniature wind-ups.
145A.
Buttons the Dog: Wind-up and battery versions (1A).
The wind-up's ears, tail, and paw move, but he's not
controlled by pushing buttons.
145B.
King Kong: This wind-up version is not remote
controlled, as is the battery toy (62B). His action is just
as nice, however, as he walks, beating his chest,
opening his mouth and growling.

There are a number of other wind-up (or friction) versions of battery toys that are not pictured here.
Some of the battery toys that have miniature versions are: Jolly Penguin (3B), Reading Bear (9B), Bear
Chef (11F), Mr. Fox Magician (20C), Picnic Bunny (21A), Drinking Bear (21D), Jocko the Drinking
Monkey (24C), Mr. Traffic Policeman (40B), Peppermint Twist Doll (49A), Hoop Zing Girl (49C),
Rollerskating Clown (54E), Exxon Tiger (57A), Disney Acrobat (63A), Santa Claus (68A), Golden Bat
(74C), Godzilla (76E), Robby the Robot (89B) and Dalek (110A).

BOXES

With many collectibles, buying an item with its original box is a bonus. Some battery toy collectors have taken that a step further. They simply will not buy a toy that does not have its original box. This may seem unreasonable, but the fact is that most Japanese toy boxes are nice enough to collect in their own right. They are colorful and attractive, with great artwork. Sometimes the box is more interesting than the toy itself. When stacked together like a jigsaw puzzle, the boxes can form a very striking display.

In addition to being beautiful, some of the boxes are functional as well. Mr. Baseball Jr.'s box stops the balls hit by the batter and separates them into hits or outs. The Gorilla Target Game's box opens into a beautifully lithographed backdrop to catch the darts shot at the toy. Whether the Japanese boxes were functional or not, it seems like much more time and effort went into designing them than went into their rivals from other countries.

On the following pages are just a few of the boxes that are considered attractive enough by some to be collectible in their own right. So, the next time you're buying a mint-in-box battery toy, just think; you're getting two items for the price of one.

A typical group of battery toy boxes. Each is beautifully designed and colored, and certainly did their job of attracting prospective buyers.

This illustrates how each year a "new and improved" toy could hit the toy shelves. Just change the name and perhaps the picture on the box, and you'd be all set. Of course, all three robots have identical actions.

Marx was particularly adept at designing interesting boxes to hold their toys.

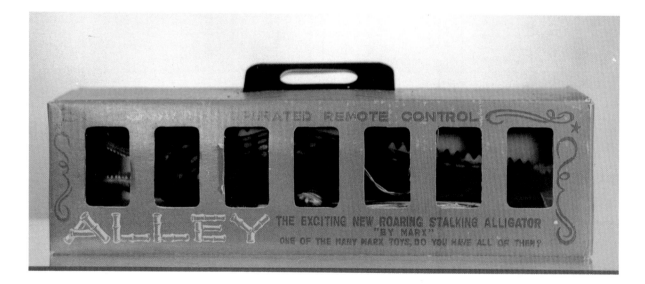

Another Marx product, Alley the Alligator's box doubles as a cage or carrying case.

What better way to sell a toy than to get a famous movie star's face on the package?

This box, designed for the Japanese market, shows a city's destruction in minute detail.

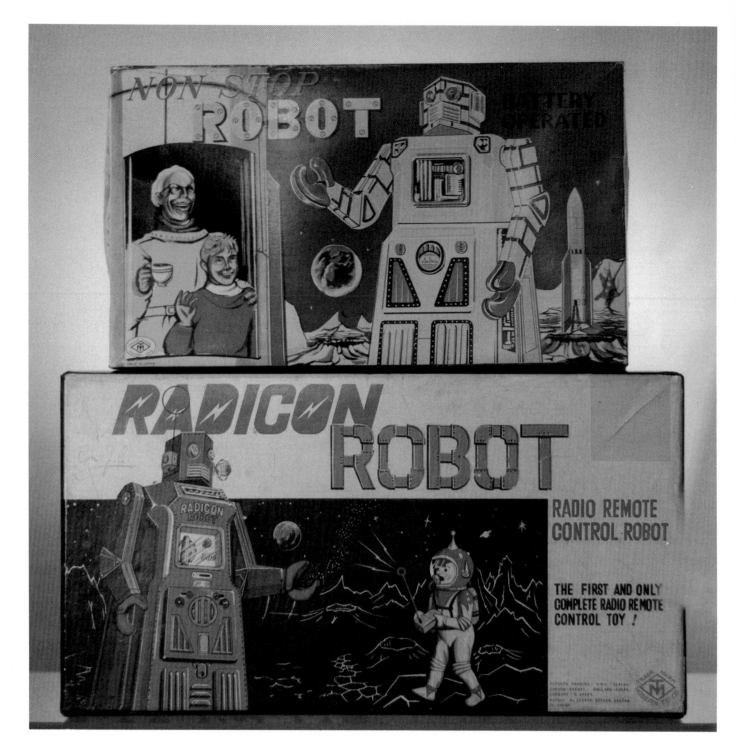

Robots were usually pictured as giants, at least twice
the size of their human masters.

The art work was not confined to the front of the box.
As you can see, the fronts and sides of these boxes are
designed differently.

159

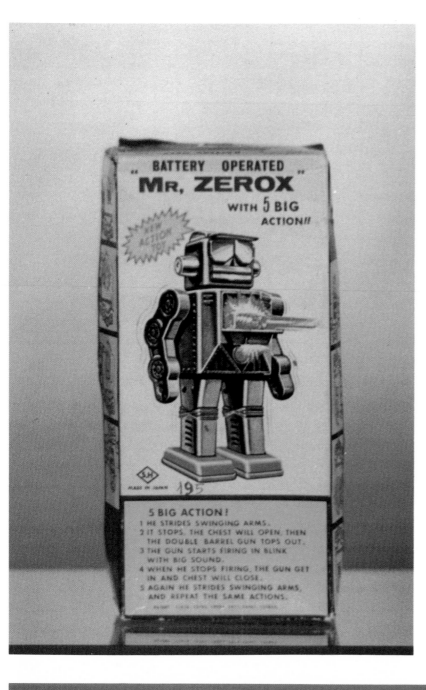

While the Japanese were masters at making unique toys with great boxes, they did sometimes have trouble explaining exactly what these toys would do.

DESIRABILITY CHART

What makes a toy desirable? If you ask ten different people, you may well get ten different responses. To some it's an intricate action, to others an attractive look. As mentioned before, rarity, subject matter and unique design are all important factors in determining a toy's desirability. The material of construction is an important consideration to many collectors, who only want tin toys. Yet some of the early plastic battery operated toys are just as eagerly sought. This is particularly true in Robots, where the late plastic robots (70's and 80's) are not very valuable, but the earlier examples, such as the Marx Electric Robot and Son (#87A;, the Mike Robot (#100E), and the Laughing Robot (#109A) are among the most popular. I personally believe that all of the above combine to make a toy desirable.

The desirability column in this chart is here to give you, as collectors, an idea of which toys are most popular within their specific field. While this is not a price guide, you will probably find that within each group (Robots, Animals, Banks, etc.) the toys with matching ratings will have similar values. For example, two #3 rated Animals will usually be close in price. This will *not* hold true when comparing toys from different groups. A #5 rated Robot *today* sells for substantially more than a #5 rated Animal or Person. Comparing Robots to any other battery toy category is like comparing apples to oranges.

By using four criteria: rarity, action, appearance, and subject matter, I've rated each toy on a scale of one to six. The numbers have the following meanings:

1 - Very common, and not particularly desired by collectors.
2 - Fairly common, but of *some* interest to collectors.
3 - Toys that are desired by *most* collectors although they are still fairly common.
4 - Very popular toys that are not quite rare but are more difficult to come by than those rated 1 through 3.
5 - Very desirable and hard to find toys.
6 - Extremely desirable toys that feature the best aspects of battery toys: rarity, great action, attractive look, and unusual subject matter.

When referring to this chart (or any other antique guide for that matter), please use it as a helpful tool in determining a toy's worth, not as a Bible. Believe me, there are no divinely inspired thoughts printed here. These are just one man's opinion, so please treat them as such.

The "Comment" portion of this chart is a grab bag of information. If a toy has a mechanical problem common to many or all of its kind, it will be mentioned here. Known variations not pictured in this book will also be listed in this column. In fact, any miscellaneous bit of trivia, fact or opinion; could appear under the "Comment" heading.

Size is another column featured in this chart. These measurements are meant to give you a general idea of a toy's size. While most sizes are fairly accurate, a few of the exact measurements were not available at the time of this writing, so they had to be approximated. While I did this to the best of my ability, and I feel that these sizes are accurate to the nearest inch, a few of the toys may be an inch or two off. I apologize for this possibility beforehand, and hope that you can all forgive me.

The toys in this chart appear in the same order that they occur in the photo section of the book. This should make cross reference easy.

I have also included in the chart a few of the more important toys that are not pictured in this book. They are listed in whichever sections they would belong, and usually with related toys. (Example: The Popeye Rowboat is in the Character Toy section right under the Smoking Popeye.)

In conclusion, let me again express the wish that this chart and the book on the whole, is helpful to you. I've tried to make it useful and enjoyable for both beginner and advanced battery toy enthusiasts. If you have any further comments or questions, feel free to contact me at: PO Box 346, Northport, New York, 11768. Also, if you know of any unusual toys that are not mentioned here, I'd appreciate it if you'd drop me a line, to let me know about them. Happy hunting.

No.	NAME	SIZE	COMMENTS	DESIRABILITY
1A.	Buttons the Dog	h.12"	Very difficult to fix.	4
1B.	Dancing Merry Chimp	h.11"		3
2A.	Talking Parrot	h.18"	Often needs new tape for recorder	5
2B.	Pretty Peggy Parrot	h.12"	Also comes in green variation.	4
2C.	Flutterbirds	h.27"		3
3A.	Circus Elephant	l.8"		2
3B.	Jolly Penguin	h.7"		3
3C.	Chippy the Chipmunk	l.9"		2
3D.	Dalmation	h.9"		1
3E.	Scottie	h.8"		1
3F.	Dachshund	l.10"	Most remote control dogs are equal in value.	1
4A.	Rooster	h.7"		3
4B.	Singing Bird			3
4C.	Singing Bird	h.9"	Both usually don't whistle.	3
4D.	Duck	h.7"		2
4E.	Worried Mother Duck	h.7"		3
5A.	Pet Turtle	l.8"	Gears sometimes slip.	2
5B.	Alley the Alligator	l.18"		4
5C.	Circus Lion	h.9½"	Often missing blanket & wand.	4
5D.	Bengali Tiger	l.12"		3
6A.	Gorilla	h.6"		4
6B.	Yeti	h.11"	Nice litho on remote control.	5
6C.	Gorilla	h.9"	Also comes in brown variation.	5
6D.	Roaring Gorilla	h.9"	Sometimes missing target gun.	4
7A.	Caterpillar	l.16"		4
7B.	Pat the Roaring Elephant	l.9"	Plastic pinion gear.	4
7C.	Baby Bertha	h.10"	The bellows usually need replacing.	4
8A.	Balloon Blowing Monkey	h.11"	Usually doesn't have enough air pressure to inflate the balloon.	4
8B.				3
8C.	Balloon Blowing Teddy	h.11"	Usually doesn't have enough air pressure to inflate the balloon.	3
8D.				4
8E.	Grandpa Bear	h.9"		4
9A.	Blacksmith Bear	h.9"		3
9B.	Reading Bear	h.9"		4
9C.	Dentist Bear	h.9½"		5
9D.	Barber Bear	h.9½"	Sometimes missing the mirror.	5
9E.	Beauty Parlor Bear	h.9½"	Rarest of the series.	5
10A.	Barney Drumming Bear	h.10"	Also a brown variation.	3
10B.	Peter Drumming Rabbit	h.12"	Also a pink variation.	3
10C.	Musical Bear	h.10"		4
10D.	Drummer Bear	h.10"	Hard to find variations	4
10E.	Musical Jackal	h.10"		4
10F.	Musical Bear	h.10"		4
11A.	Hoopy the Fishing Duck	h.10"	Sometimes missing the fish.	4
11B.				
11C.	Fishing Bear	h.10"	Sometimes missing the fish.	4
11D.	Piggy Cook	h.10½"	Sometimes missing egg & hat.	3
11E.	Doggy Chef	h.9"	Sometimes missing the hamburger.	4
11F.	Bear Chef	h.10"	Sometimes missing the egg.	5
12A.				4
12B.	Telephone Bear	h.7"		4
12C.	VIP Busy Boss Bear	h.8"	Usually missing table lamp.	4
12D.	Bear Cashier	h.7"		4
not shown	Rabbit Cashier	h.7"	Variation of 12D.	4
13A.	Music Hall	h.7½"	Sometimes needs a rubber belt inside replaced.	4
13B.				4
13C.	Jolly Pianist	h.8"		4
13D.	Musical Bulldog	h.9"		6
14A.				5
14B.	Rock 'n' Roll Monkey	h.11"	Sometimes missing hat.	5
14C.				3
14D.	Bongo Monkey	h.9½"	Sometimes missing hat.	3
15A.				4
15B.	Sneezing Bear	h.9"		4
15C.	Knitting Grandma	h.8"		4
15D.	Monkey Artist	h.8"		4
15E.	Busy Housekeeper Bear	h.8½"		4
16A.	Telephone Rabbit	h.9"		4
16B.				4
16C.	Telephone Bear	h.9"	Also a rocking chair variation.	4
16D.	Papa Bear	h.9"		4
16E.	Birdwatcher Bear	h.9"	Different clothing variations.	5
16F.	Mother Bear	h.9"		4
17A.	Bubbleblowing Elephant	h.7"	Usually doesn't blow bubbles. Plastic cup sometimes missing.	2
17B.	Bubble Blowing Rabbit	h.7"	Usually doesn't blow bubbles. Plastic cup sometimes missing.	3
17C.	Bubble Blowing Kangaroo	h.7½"	Usually doesn't blow bubbles. Baby often missing ears.	4
17D.	Bubbles Washing Bear	h.8"	Usually doesn't make bubbles.	4
17E.	Bubble Blowing Monkey	h.10"		2
17F.	Bubble Blowing Dog	h.7½"	Sometimes doesn't blow bubbles. Cup sometimes missing.	4
18A.	Royal Cub	h.8"		4
18B.	Rabbit Carriage	h.8"	Different color variations.	4
18C.	Hungry Baby Bear	h.9"		4
18D.	Hungry Baby Pup	h.9"	Much rarer than 18C.	4
18E.	Spanking Bear	h.9"	Mama's hand often brittle.	5
19A.				4
19B.	Playful Dog	l.7"		4
19C.	Lion Target Game	h.7"	Rubber tail sometimes breaks.	4
19D.	Bubble Blowing Lion	h.7"	Sometimes doesn't blow bubbles. Rubber tail sometimes breaks.	3
20A.	Bear Target Game	h.9"	Sometimes missing gun.	4
20B.	Bubble Blowing Bear	h.9"	Sometimes doesn't blow bubbles.	4
20C.	Mr. Fox Magician	h.9"	Sometimes missing the rabbit.	4
20D.	Mr. Fox Magician	h.9"	Usually doesn't blow bubbles.	4
21A.				3
21B.				3
21C.	Picnic Bunny	h.10"	A rubber tube running thru the body usually needs replacing.	3
21D.	Drinking Bear)			3
21E.	Drinking Monkey)	all 9½"	All usually need the rubber	
21F.	Drinking Panda Bear)		tube that goes thru the body replaced.	
22A.	Mambo the Drumming Elephant)			4
22B.	Dandy the Drumming Dog)		Also a black variation.	3
22C.	Daisy the Drumming Duck)			4
22D.	Peter the Drumming Rabbit)		Also a pink variation.	4
22E.	Dalmation one man band)			4
22F.	Chimpy the Drumming Monkey)	all 9"		4
23A.	Shoemaker Bear	h.8"		4
23B.	Shoeshine Monkey	h.8"		3
23C.	Shoeshine Bear	h.8"		4
23D.	Smoking Elephant)			4
23E.	Mr. Mc Pooch)			4
23F.	Smoking Papa Bear)	All 8½"		3
23G.	Smoking Rabbit	h.9"		3
24A.	Bobby the Drinking Bear	h.10"	Also a white variation.	4
24B.	Jocko the Drinking Monkey	h.10")	On both, the tube leading	4
24C.	Jocko the Drinking Monkey	h.11")	from the mouth sometimes needs replacing.	4
24D.	Drinking Dog	h.9"		3
24E.	Drinking Dog	h.7"		3
24F.	Maxwell Coffee Loving Bear	h.9"	Light under the coffee pot is sometimes out.	4
25A.	Traveler Bear	h.8"		4
25B.	Sleeping Baby Bear	l.8½"	Often missing the alarm clock.	4
25C.	Teddy the Artist	h.9"	Should include nine different templates.	5
25D.	Susie the Cashier Bear	h.8½"	Items are sometimes missing from the conveyor belt.	5
26A.	Teddy Go Cart	h.10½"	Usually needs a new pinion gear.	3
26B.	Cappy the Baggage Porter	h.12"		4

h.=height   l.=length

No.	NAME	SIZE	COMMENTS	DESIRABILITY
26C	Chimp and Pup Railcar	h.8"		4
26D	Penguin on Tricycle	h.6½"		4
27A	Popcorn Vendor Bear	h.8½"	Should have a tin sign on his back.	4
not shown	Popcorn Vendor Rabbit	h.9"	Variation of 27A.	5
27B	Mac the Turtle	h.8"		4
27C	Jolly Bear Peanut Vendor	h.8"	Smokestack and hat sometimes missing.	4
27D	Popcorn Vendor Duck	h.7"		4
28A	Yum Yum Kitty	h.9"		5
28B	Jolly Bambino	h.9"		4
28C	Picnic Monkey	h.9"		5
28D	Suzette the Eating Monkey	h.9"	Steak sometimes missing.	5
28E	Hungry Cat	h.8"	Should have pink plastic "goldfish".	5
29A	Professor Owl	h.7"	Comes with 2 picture discs.	4
29B	Ball Playing Bear	h.9½"	Has fragile celluloid parts.	4
29C	Jungle Trio	h.7½"	Rubber arms and legs break easily.	6
29D	Feeding Bird Watcher	h.8½"	Plastic feet on Mama sometimes broken. Branch on tree often missing.	5
30A	Saxaphone Monkey	h.9½"	Drum often missing.	5
30B	Trumpet Monkey	h.9½"		4
30C	Accordion Bear	h.10½"		5
30D	Bruno the Accordion Bear	h.10½"		4
31A	Frankie the Rollerskating Monkey	h.12"	Hat sometimes missing. Also a skiing variation.	4
31B	Big John	h.12"		2
31C	Yo-Yo Monkey	h.9"		4
31D	Friendly Jocko	h.8"	Should come with cymbals and cup.	4
31E	Crapshooting Monkey	h.8½"	Visor sometimes missing.	2
32A	Bunny Magician	h.12"	Several color variations.	4
32B	Windy	h.10"	Sometimes missing umbrella or ball.	3
32C	Lady Pup Gardener	h.8"	Very fragile.	5
32D	Tricky Dog House	h.6"		2
32E	Ball Playing Dog	h.8"		4
33A	Teddy the Boxing Bear	h.9"		4
33B	Jolly Bear	h.7"		3
33C	Cine Bear	h.11"	Usually missing plastic worms.	5
33D	Shoeshine Bear	h.10½"		4
33E	Shooting Bear	h.10"		4
34A	Teddy Bear Swing	h.18"		5
34B	Hy Que Monkey	h.18"	Difficult to fix.	5
35A	Monkey Car	h.7"		4
35B	Trumpet Playing Rabbit	h.10"	Several color variations.	4
35C	Hippo Chef	h.10"	Sometimes missing hamburger.	5
not shown	Elephant Chef	h.10"	Sometimes missing hamburger.	5
35D	Popcorn Bear	h.9"		4
35E	Drinking Cat	h.10"		4
36A	Mr. Strongpup	h.9"		5
36B	Champion Weight Lifter	h.9"		1
36C	Mighty Mike	h.12"	Barbells should light.	3
36D	Happy Band Trio	h.12"		4
37A	Mischievious Monkey	h.12"		4
37B	Clown and Lion	h.12"		5
37C	Charm the Cobra	h.6"	Flute sometimes missing	3
37D	Pipie the Whale	l.12"	Rubber fins often missing.	3
38A	Funland Cup Ride	h.8"		2
38B	Serpent Charmer	h.7"		5
39A	Calypso Joe	h.11"	Hat & ears sometimes missing.	5
39B	Nutty Nibs	h.12"	Difficult to take apart. Nut tray often missing.	6
40A	Major Tootie	h.12"		3
40B	Mr. Traffic Policeman	h.13"		4
40C	Shaving Sam	h.12"	Mirror sometimes missing.	4
40D	Happy Miner	h.11"		4
40E	Cycling Daddy	h.10"		4
41A	Playboy	h.12"		4
41B	Charlie Weaver Bartender	h.11½"	Plastic glass breaks easily. Ice cubes sometimes missing.	3
41C	Good Time Charlie	h.12"	Has some diecast internal parts which break easily.	3
41D	Crapshooter	h.9"	Has a diecast gear.	2
not shown	Roulette Man	h.9"	Has a diecast gear.	4
41E	Chef Cook	h.10½"	Sometimes missing the omlette and hat.	4
42A	Pinkee the Farmer	h.9"	One of a series of comical vehicular toys.	4
42B	Kissing Couple	h.10"		4
42C	Bubble Blowing Boy	h.7"	Usually doesn't blow bubbles. Plastic bubble solution cup often missing.	3
42D	Bubble Blowing Musician	h.11"	Usually doesn't blow bubbles. Cup sometimes missing.	4
42E	Snake Charmer	h.7"	Plastic snake or basket sometimes damaged or missing.	4
43A	El Toro	h.9½"	Bull often does not smoke properly.	4
43B	Wild West Rodeo	h.6"	Sometimes doesn't blow bubbles. Bubble solution cup sometimes missing.	4
43C	Dog Sled	l.14"		5
not shown	Santa Sled	l.14"	Variation of 43C.	5
44A	Overland Stage	l.14"		4
44B	Cowboy on Horse	h.7"		4
44C	Stagecoach	l.13"		4
45A	Nutty Mad Indian	h.12"	Top of drum often torn.	4
45B	Red Gulch Bar	h.10"		5
45C	Pistol Pete	h.12"	Hat sometimes missing.	4
45D	Dancing Indian	h.10"		3
45E	Two Gun Sheriff	h.10"	Hat sometimes missing.	3
46A	Girl with Baby Carriage	h.8"		4
46B	Dolly Seamstress	h.7"		4
46C	Busy Secretary	h.7"		4
46D	Miss Friday Typist	h.7"		4
not shown	Telephone Operator	h.7"	In same series as 46D.	5
47A	Telephone Linesman	h.4"	(figure only)-Seldom works smoothly.	4
47B	Climbing Fireman	h.6½"	(figure only)	4
47C	Climbing Fireman	h.6½"	(figure only)	4
47D	Ol' Sleepy Head Rip	h.8½"	Blue bird sometimes missing.	4
47E	Smoking Grandpa	h.9"		4
48A	Bartender	h.11½"	Plastic "glass" is fragile. Ice cubes sometimes missing. Also a "Rolling Eyes" variation.	2
48B	Blushing Willie	h.10"	Has a plastic pinion gear.	1
48C	Drinking Captain	h.12"		3
48D	Mc Gregor	h.11"	Sometimes won't stand up.	4
48E	Puffy Morris	h.10"	Usually will not blow smoke.	4
48F	Pat O'Neill	h.11"	Usually won't work properly.	4
49A	Peppermint Twist Doll	h.12"		4
49B	My Fair Dancer	h.9"		3
49C	Hoop Zing Girl	h.10½"	Celluloid parts are fragile.	4
49D	Mr. Baseball Jr.	h.7"	Bat tends to break.	4
49E	Dancing Sweethearts	h.7"	Celluloid heads are fragile.	4
49F	Shutterbug	h.8½"	Usually needs rubber O ring replaced.	4
50A	Sammy Wong	h.10"	All look alike.	4
50B	Strutting Sam	h.10½"		5
50C	Gino the Balloon Man	h.10"	Bubble cup sometimes missing.	4
50D	Mexicali Pete	h.11"		3
50E	Indian Joe	h.11"	One of many Indian drummer toys.	2
50F	Mumbo Jumbo	h.10"		3
51A	Clown and Monkey Car	h.8"	Monkey is often missing hat.	4
51B	Clown on Unicycle	h.10½"		5

h.=height   l.=length

No.	NAME	SIZE	COMMENTS	DESIRABILITY
51C.	Comic Jumping Jeep	l.12″	Usually needs plastic pinion gear replaced.	2
51D.	Happy Clown Car	l.6″		2
52A.	Magic Man	h.12″		5
52B.	Clown Magician	h.11″	Card trick sometimes doesn't function properly.	4
52C.	Clown Circus Car	h.9″	His coat fades quickly.	4
52D.	Cyclist Clown	h.6½″		4
53A.	Blinky the Clown	h.10½″	Paper hat often missing.	5
53B.	Bimbo the Clown	h.9″	Sometimes missing felt hat.	4
53C.	Happy/Sad Clown	h.9½″		4
53D.	Charlie the Drumming Clown	h.9″	Several clothing variations.	4
53E.	Musical Clown	h.9″		5
54A.	Pinky the Clown	h.10″		4
54B.	Bingo Clown	h.13″		3
54C.	Balloon Vendor	h.13″	Bell or balloons sometimes missing.	4
54D.	Acrobat Clown	h.9″		3
54E.	Roller Skating Clown	h.6″	Coat fades quickly.	5
55A.	High Jinx at the Circus	h.10″	The gear that controls the ladder breaks under the stress of working the toy.	4
55B.	Hobo Playing Accordion	h.10″	Green coat fades quickly.	5
55C.	Yo-Yo Clown	h.9″		4
55D.	Happy the Clown Puppet Show	h.10″		4
56A.	Laughing Clown	h.14″		4
56B.	Dozo the Steaming Clown	h.14″		4
56C.	Ball Blowing Clown	h.12″	Clothing fades quickly, air sometimes not functioning.	4
56D.	Happy the Violinist	h.10″	Violin sometimes missing.	5
57A.	Esso Tiger	h.11″	Often missing hat and flowers.	5
57B.	Walking Batman	h.11½″	Made for the Japanese market.	5
58A.	Smokey Bear	h.8½″		4
58B.	Smokey the Bear Jeep	l.10″		5
58C.	Batman Car	l.8″	Made for the Japanese market.	4
58D.	Batman	h.10″	Made for the Japanese market.	5
58E.	Batmobile	l.11″		2
59A.	Rocky	h.3½″	Unlicensed Flintstone toy.	1
59B.	Fred Flintstone's Bedrock Band	h.9″		4
59C.	Fred Flintstone on Dino	l.18″	Colors fade easily. Whistle sometimes doesn't work.	4
60A.	Secret Agent Car	l.10″	Man who is ejected sometimes missing.	4
60B.	Monkeymobile	l.11″		4
not shown	Arthur A Go-Go	h.9″	Unlicensed "Beatles" Drummer toy.	5
60C.	Fred Flintstone Car	l.6″		4
61A.	Topo Gigio Playing the Xylophone	h.8″		5
61B.	Topo Gigio	h.11″		4
61C.	Pinnochio Playing the Xylophone	h.8″		3
61D.	Dennis the Menace Playing the Xylophone.	h.8″		4
62A.	Superman Tank	l.10″		5
62B.	Mighty Kong	h.11″		5
62C.	Tarzan	h.13″	Often does not walk well.	4
63A.	Disney Acrobat	h.9″	Celluloid parts crack easily.	4
not shown	Disney Fire Engine		Great Linemar toy—Donald climbs up the ladder—often missing parts.	5
63B.	Pluto Lantern	h.6″	Rubber tongue and tail sometimes cracked or missing.	3
63C.	Donald Duck	h.8″		2
63D.	Pluto	l.10″		4
64A.	Mickey Mouse Drummer	h.11″		5
64B.	Bubble Blowing Popeye	h.12″	Watch for corrosion around the mouth.	5
64C.	Mickey Magician	h.10″	Chick is often missing.	6
64D.	Smoking Popeye	h.7½″		5
not shown	Popeye in Rowboat		Very rare tin R.C. Linemar toy.	6
65A.	Popeye Paddlewagon	l.7″		3
65B.	Popeye Lantern	h.6″		3
65C.	Mr. Magoo Car	l.9″	Battery case often corroded.	4
65D.	Tom and Jerry Train	l.9½″		3
65E.	Mickey Mouse Handcar	h.8″		4
66A.	Tom and Jerry Jumping Jeep	l.9″		3
66B.	Tom and Jerry Highway Patrol	l.8″		3
66C.	Tom Handcar	h.8″		3
66D.	Jerry Handcar	h.8″		3
67A.	Tweety and Sylvester Alarm Clock	h.8″		2
67B.	Snoopy Dog House	h.8″		1
67C.	Pluto	h.8″		1
67D.	Spiderman Car	l.6″		1
67E.	Drumming Pink Panther	h.10″		1
68A.	Santa Claus	h.12″		3
68B.	Santa on the Globe	h.14½″	Very difficult to repair.	5
68C.	Santa Claus	h.12″	Hard to find variation.	4
69A.	Santa Claus	h.18″		5
69B.	Santa in Rocker	h.21″	Stocking sometimes missing. Tree is fragile.	5
70A.	Happy Santa	h.9″		4
70B.	Happy Santa	h.11″	Celluloid face cracks easily.	4
70C.	Santa Scooter	h.8″		2
70D.	Santa Handcar	h.8″		3
71A.	Snowman	h.11½″	Air often not functioning. Pipe usually missing.	4
71B.	Skiing Santa	h.12″	Skis often missing.	4
71C.	Santa on Roof	h.7″		3
71D.	Santa Claus	h.10″		5
72A.	Haunted House	h.10″	Very difficult to repair.	5
73A.	Laffun Head	h.7″	Many variations.	2
73B.	Tiger Plaque	h.10″		4
73C.				
73D.	Holiday Lanterns	h.5″	Many variations.	2
74A.	Creeping Crawling Hand	l.8″	Vinyl skin is usually brittle and cracked or melted.	5
74B.	Nutty Mad Car	l.9″	Hubcaps sometimes missing.	4
74C.	Golden Bat	h.11½″		5
74D.	Knight in Armor	h.12″	Bow and arrow sometimes missing.	4
74E.	??????????	h.11″	God knows what's missing.	5
75A.				
75B.	Whistling Tree	h.15″	Sometimes doesn't whistle.	6
76A.	Walking Frankenstein	h.12½″	Sometimes doesn't bend due to a broken die cast cam.	6
76B.	Prehistoric Monster	h.10″		4
76C.	Barragon	h.12″		4
76D.	Jiras	h.12″		4
76E.	Godzilla	h.12″		4
not shown	Gaigon	h.12″	Hardest to find in the Godzilla series.	5
77A.	Mod Monster	h.12″	Die cast ring that holds the pants sometimes breaks.	4
77B.	Turn Signal Frankenstein	h.6″		4
77C.	Frankenstein	h.12½″	Die cast ring that holds pants sometimes breaks.	4
78A.	Snappy the Dragon	l.30″	Fades easily. Difficult to repair.	6
79A.	Santa on Roof Bank	h.10½″		4
79B.	Santa at Desk Bank	h.8″	Pencil sometimes missing.	5
80A.	Fishing Bears Bank	l.8″	Fish often missing.	6
80B.	Cowboy Savings Bank	h.8″		4
80C.	Globe Explorer Bank	h.10″	Should have a rocket and a saucer.	6

164

h.=height   l.=length

No.	NAME	SIZE	COMMENTS	DESIRABILITY
81A.	Clown Vending Machine Bank	h.10″		5
81B.	Organ Grinder Bank	h.9″	Monkey often missing.	5
81C.	Gypsy Witch Fortune Teller Bank	h.11″	Should have a series of fortune cards.	6
82A.	Red Cab Bank	l.9½″		2
82B.	Yellow Cab Bank	l.8½″		4
82C.	Pepsi Vending Machine Bank	h.10″		4
82D.	Coca Cola Vending Machine Bank	h.10″		4
83A.	The Hand from Uncle Bank	h.5″	Plastic pinion gear.	3
83B.	Eightball Bank	h.7″	Plastic pinion gear.	4
83C.	Down the Drain Bank	h.5½″	Plastic pinion gear.	3
83D.	Clown Bank	h.9½″	Plastic parts often crack.	3
83E.	Bartender Bank	l.10″		3
84A.	Uncle Sam High Taxes Bank	l.9″	Plastic pinion gear.	3
84B.	Hole in One Bank	l.9″	Plastic pinion gear.	2
84C.				2
84D.	Bowling Bank	l.11″	Plastic pinion gear.	2
85A.	Luncheonette Bank	h.8″	Should have plastic utensils.	4
85B.	Treasure Chest Bank	h.10½″	Very difficult to fix.	3
85C.	Gofer Bank	h.6″		3
86A.	Haunted House Bank	h.6″		3
86B.	Haunted House Bank	h.8″		3
86C.	Tweety and Sylvester Bank	h.9″		1
86D.	Buddy L Mickey Mouse Disco Bank	h.7″		3
87A.	Electric Robot and Son	h.14½″	Tools and son sometimes missing. Often runs sluggishly.	4
87B.	Answer Game	h.15″	Comes with pad and pencil.	4
88A.	Mechanized Robot	l.13″		6
89A.				6
89B.	Robbie the Robot	h.12½″	Dome often cracked. Rubber hands are sometimes missing.	5
89C.	Planet Robot	h.9″		4
89D.	Space Trooper	h.6″		5
89E.	Robbie	h.8½″	Dome sometimes cracked.	5
90A.	Man in Space	l.7″	Very fragile.	4
90B.	Robot	h.7½″		5
91A.	Colonel HAP Hazard	h.12″	Facemask sometimes cracked. Antenna sometimes missing.	4
91B.	High Bounce Moon Scout	h.12″	Facemask sometimes cracked. Antenna sometimes missing.	5
91C.	Earthman	h.9″		5
91D.	Spaceman	h.7″		5
91E.	Astronaut	h.9″	Gun sometimes broken.	5
92A.				5
92B.			Hardest version to find.	5
92C.	Astronaut	h.13″	Antenna is usually missing or has been replaced.	5
93D.	Remote Control Astronaut	h.7½″		4
92E.	Spaceman	h.7″		5
93A.	Cragstan Astronaut	h.14″	Vinyl hands are sometimes off and the dome is sometimes cracked.	6
93B.	Great Astronaut	h.15″		5
93C.	Astronaut	h.14″	Same as 93A.	6
94A.	Missile M Robot	h.17″	Antenna sometimes missing.	5
94B.	Moon Explorer	h.18″	Antenna sometimes missing.	5
94C.	Rocket Man	h.16″	Antenna sometimes missing. Rockets usually missing.	5
95A.	Train Robot	h.15″		6
95B.	Target Robot	h.15″	Gun sometimes missing.	6
96A.	Lavender Robot	h.15″		5
96B.	Radicon Robot	h.15″	Remote control sometimes missing. Very fragile mechanism.	6
97A.	Mr. Robot	h.10″		4
97B.	Jupiter Robot	h.12″		5
97C.	Modern Robot	h.10″		4

No.	NAME	SIZE	COMMENTS	DESIRABILITY
97D.	Mighty Robot	h.11″	Plastic head sometimes damaged.	5
97E.	Chief Smoky	h.11″		5
97F.	Chief Robot Man	h.11″	Many color variations.	5
98A.				4
98B.				4
98C.	Zoomer	h.8″	Many color variations.	4
98D.	Radar Robot	h.9″		5
98E.	Musical Drumming Robot	h.8″		5
99A.	Wheelbarrow Robot	h.12″	Wheelbarrow sometimes missing.	4
99B.	Forklift Robot	h.12″	The box he carries is often missing.	5
99C.	Original Lost in Space Robot	h.12″	Bottom plate that holds batteries is sometimes broken. Head is usually split.	3
99D.	Lost in Space Robot	h.10″		2
100A.	Gigantor	h.8½″		3
100B.	Robot Control	h.7″		4
100C.	Golden Roto Robot	h.8½″	Legs sometimes cracked where they are attached to the body.	2
100D.	Talking Robot	h.10″	Talk is sometimes garbled.	4
100E.	Mike Robot	h.12″	Microphone often doesn't work.	4
100F.	Piston Head Robot	h.9″		3
101A.	Moonlight Man	h.12″	One of a large series of Japanese super heros.	3
101B.	Mat Astronaut	h.12″		3
101C.	Millerman	h.13″		3
101D.	Astronaut	h.14″	Dome sometimes cracked or missing.	4
101E.	Gigantor	h.13″		5
102A.	Smoking Spaceman	h.12″	Smoke sometimes not working.	5
102B.	Wheel - A - Gear Robot	h.16″	Rubberband in chest usually needs replacing.	5
not shown	Blink - A - Gear Robot		Variation of 102B	4
102C.	Rosko Astronaut	h.12½″	The dome is sometimes cracked and the buzzer doesn't always work.	5
103A.				
103B.	Mr. Mercury	h.12½″	The foam handpads are often worn, and an easily broken die cast gear controls bending.	5
103C.	Space Explorer	h.12″	Extremely difficult to repair. Several variations.	5
103D.	Mr. Atomic	h.9″	Dome is sometimes cracked. Also a blue variation.	6
104A.	Robotank Z	h.10″	Plastic pinion gear.	4
Not shown	Talking Robotank Z	h.10″	Variation of 104A, speaks Japanese.	4
not shown	Robotank R-1	h.10″	Earlier version of 104A.	3
104B.	Space Commander	h.10″		3
104C.	Thunder Robot	h.12″	Antenna is sometimes missing	5
104D.	Dino	h.12″	Head sometimes sticks in the open position.	4
105A.				5
105B.	Directional Robot	h.10½″		5
105C.	Radar Robot	h.11″		5
105D.	Robot	h.9″		5
105E.	Robot 8	h.12″	Pinion gear sometimes needs replacing.	5
106A.	Mini Robotank	h.4½″	Has a plastic pinion gear.	3
106B.	Walking Robot	h.6″	The dome is very fragile. Also an undomed variation.	4
106C.	Mini Robotank TR2	h.4½″	Has a plastic pinion gear.	3
106D.	Powder Robot	h.7½″		5
106E.	Robot	h.6″		5
106F.	Mr. Robot Mechanical Brain	h.8″		4
107A.	Engine Robot	h.8½″	Several variations.	3

h.=height   l.=length

165

No.	NAME	SIZE	COMMENTS	DESIRABILITY
107B.	Robot	h.9″	Also a silver version.	4
107C.	Space Scout	h.8½″	Also a silver variation.	4
not shown	Mr. Xerox	h.8½″	Robot version of 107C.	4
107D.	Gear Robot	h.11″	The plastic front is sometimes cracked.	4
107E.	Mr. Patrol	h.11″		4
not shown	Robot version of Mr. Patrol	h.11″	Similar to 107E.	5
107F.	Turn Signal Robot	h.11″	Plastic front sometimes cracks.	4
108A.	Robot Commando	h.20″	Has many parts which may be missing.	2
108B.	Pepo	h.30″		4
109A.	Hysterical Harry	h.13″		3
109B.	Giant Robot	h.14″		3
109C.	Mr. Lem	h.13″		2
109D.	Gear Robot	h.12½″		2
109E.	Krome Dome	h.11″		3
109F.	Lunar Spaceman	h.11½″		2
110A.	Dalek	h.6″	American batteries are slightly too large for the battery box. Several variations.	3
110B.	Tiny Robot	h.4″		3
110C.	Talking Dalek	h.6″	From *Dr. Who* T.V. show.	2
not shown	Talking K-9 (Robot Dog.)		Also from *Dr. Who.*	2
110D.	Explo	h.7½″		2
110E.	Mr. Brain	l.10″		3
110F.	Jupiter Robot	h.6″		3
111A.	Missile Robot	h.9″	One of a large series of 70's Robots.	1
111B.	Mr. Monster	h.11″		1
111C.	Mr. Mercury	h.10″	One of a series of 70's Robots.	1
111D.	Space Explorer	h.12″	Many different versions.	2
111E.	Attacking Martian	h.10″	One of a very large series of 60's & 70's Robots.	2
111F.	Swivel - O - Matic Astronaut	h.12″	Many variations.	2
112A.	City Bus	l.14″		2
112B.	School Bus	l.13″		3
112C.	Sound Bus	l.15″		2
112D.	Sight Seeing Bus	l.9″		4
113A.	Motorcycle	l.11½″	Very complex mechanism.	5
113B.	Police Motorcycle	l.11½″	Very complex mechanism.	5
113C.	Mystery Jet Plane	l.10½″		4
113D.	Highway Patrol Car	l.15½″		4
114A.	Television Truck	l.11″		4
114B.	NBC Truck	l.8″		4
114C.	Railroad Handcar	l.10″		4
114D.	Forklift Truck	l.10″		3
115A.	Merry Go Round Truck	l.10″		4
115B.	All Trains (various sizes)		Most are very difficult to sell. Many variations.	1-2
115C.				
115D.				
115E.	All Tractors and Bulldozers (various sizes)		Many variations	1-3
116A.	All Fire Engines (various sizes)		Many variations.	1-4
116B.	Coke Truck	l.11″		4
116C.	Jeep	l.10″		2
116D.	Combat Tank	l.9″		2
117A.	Ocean Liner	l.20″		5
117B.	Aircraft Carrier	l. 20″	Many small parts sometimes missing.	5
117C.	All Speedboats (various sizes)		Many variations.	1-3
117D.	Nautilus Sub	l.14″		4
117E.	Captain Kidd Pirate Ship	l.13″		3
118A.	Mars Rocket	l.13″		4
118B.	Space Captain	l.12″		4
118C.	Cape Canaveral Truck	l.8″	Space version of NBC truck.	4

No.	NAME	SIZE	COMMENTS	DESIRABILITY
118D.	Space Survey Saucer	l.8″		4
118E.	Space Patrol Tank	l.10″		4
119A.	Piston Tractor	l.9″	Battery cases often corroded.	4
119B.	Radar Tractor	l.9″		4
119C.	Robot Tractor	l.9″		4
119D.	Space Robot Car	l.11″	Often missing parts.	5
119E.	Robot Bulldozer	l.8″		4
119F.	Robot Car X-9	l.10″	Dome sometimes cracked.	5
120A.	1960's Plymouth TV Wagon	l.12″		4
120B.	1950's Plymouth	l.11½″		4
121A.	1950's Cadillac	l.12″		6
121B.	1950's Cadillac Convertible	l.12″		5
121C.	1960's Cadillac	l.12″		4
122.	1950's Buick	l.7½″	Friction motors - Battery operated lights only.	5
123A.	1950's Thunderbird	l.11″		5
123B.	1950's Thunderbird Convertible	l.11″		6
123C.	1950's Thunderbird	l.12″		4
124A.	1960's Corvette	l.11″		5
124B.	1960's Corvette	l.10″		3
124C.	1960's Corvette	l.10″		3
125A.	1960's Mustang	l.12″		4
125B.	1960's Mustang	l.11″		4
125C.	1960's Mustang	l.10″	Racing decals detract from value.	2
126A.	1950's Benz	l.10½″		5
126B.	(See box section)			
126C.	1950's Benz Racer	l.10″		4
127A.	1960's 220 S Benz	l.11½″		5
127B.	1960's Benz	l.13″		4
127C.	1960's Benz Taxi	l.10″		4
128A.	1960's Volkswagon	l.9½″		4
128B.	1960's Bolkswagon	l.13″		4
128C.	1960's Volkswagon Convertible	l.9½″		4
128D.	1960's Volkswagon Convertible	l.13″		5
129A.	1960's Volkswagon Convertible	l.8″	Plastic pinion gear.	3
129B.	1960's Volkswagon	l.8″	Plastic pinion gear.	2
129C.	1960's Volkswagon Microbus	l.10″		4
129D.	1960's Volkswagon Pick-Up	l.8″		3
130A.	1960's Porsche	l.10″		4
130B.	1960's Porsche	l.8½″		2
130C.	1960's Jaguar	l.10″		4
131A.	1960's Rolls Royce	l.12″		5
131B.	1960's Ferrari	l.11″	Plastic pinion gear.	4
131C.	1960's Citroen	l.12″		5
132A.	1950's Opel	l.11″		5
132B.	1950's Lincoln	l.12″		5
132C.	1950's Mercury	l.9″		4
133A.	1960's Camero	l.10″		2
133B.	1960's Pontiac Firebird	l.10″		3
133C.	1960's Cougar	l.10″		2
134A.	1960's Ford	l.12″	Possibly late 1950's.	4
134B.	1960's Ford GT	l.12″		3
134C.	1960's Toronado	l.10½″		3
135A.	1960's Corvair	l.12″		4
135B.	1960's Sea Hawk	l.13″		3
135C.	1960's Ford Gyron	l.10½″	Also a red and black remote control version.	4
137A.	Great Garloo	h.24″	Usually missing medallion.	4

h.=height   l.=length

No.	NAME	SIZE	COMMENTS	DESIRABILITY
81A.	Clown Vending Machine Bank	h.10″		5
81B.	Organ Grinder Bank	h.9″	Monkey often missing.	5
81C.	Gypsy Witch Fortune Teller Bank	h.11″	Should have a series of fortune cards.	6
82A.	Red Cab Bank	l.9½″		2
82B.	Yellow Cab Bank	l.8½″		4
82C.	Pepsi Vending Machine Bank	h.10″		4
82D.	Coca Cola Vending Machine Bank	h.10″		4
83A.	The Hand from Uncle Bank	h.5″	Plastic pinion gear.	3
83B.	Eightball Bank	h.7″	Plastic pinion gear.	4
83C.	Down the Drain Bank	h.5½″	Plastic pinion gear.	3
83D.	Clown Bank	h.9½″	Plastic parts often crack.	3
83E.	Bartender Bank	l.10″		3
84A.	Uncle Sam High Taxes Bank	l.9″	Plastic pinion gear.	3
84B.	Hole in One Bank	l.9″	Plastic pinion gear.	2
84C.				2
84D.	Bowling Bank	l.11″	Plastic pinion gear.	2
85A.	Luncheonette Bank	h.8″	Should have plastic utensils.	4
85B.	Treasure Chest Bank	h.10½″	Very difficult to fix.	3
85C.	Gofer Bank	h.6″		3
86A.	Haunted House Bank	h.6″		3
86B.	Haunted House Bank	h.8″		3
86C.	Tweety and Sylvester Bank	h.9″		1
86D.	Buddy L Mickey Mouse Disco Bank	h.7″		3
87A.	Electric Robot and Son	h.14½″	Tools and son sometimes missing. Often runs sluggishly.	4
87B.	Answer Game	h.15″	Comes with pad and pencil.	4
88A.	Mechanized Robot	l.13″		6
89A.				6
89B.	Robbie the Robot	h.12½″	Dome often cracked. Rubber hands are sometimes missing.	5
89C.	Planet Robot	h.9″		4
89D.	Space Trooper	h.6″		5
89E.	Robbie	h.8½″	Dome sometimes cracked.	5
90A.	Man in Space	l.7″	Very fragile.	4
90B.	Robot	h.7½″		5
91A.	Colonel HAP Hazard	h.12″	Facemask sometimes cracked. Antenna sometimes missing.	4
91B.	High Bounce Moon Scout	h.12″	Facemask sometimes cracked. Antenna sometimes missing.	5
91C.	Earthman	h.9″		5
91D.	Spaceman	h.7″		5
91E.	Astronaut	h.9″	Gun sometimes broken.	5
92A.				5
92B.			Hardest version to find.	5
92C.	Astronaut	h.13″	Antenna is usually missing or has been replaced.	5
93D.	Remote Control Astronaut	h.7½″		4
92E.	Spaceman	h.7″		5
93A.	Cragstan Astronaut	h.14″	Vinyl hands are sometimes off and the dome is sometimes cracked.	6
93B.	Great Astronaut	h.15″		5
93C.	Astronaut	h.14″	Same as 93A.	6
94A.	Missile M Robot	h.17″	Antenna sometimes missing.	5
94B.	Moon Explorer	h.18″	Antenna sometimes missing.	5
94C.	Rocket Man	h.16″	Antenna sometimes missing. Rockets usually missing.	5
95A.	Train Robot	h.15″		6
95B.	Target Robot	h.15″	Gun sometimes missing.	6
96A.	Lavender Robot	h.15″		5
96B.	Radicon Robot	h.15″	Remote control sometimes missing. Very fragile mechanism.	6
97A.	Mr. Robot	h.10″		4
97B.	Jupiter Robot	h.12″		5
97C.	Modern Robot	h.10″		4
97D.	Mighty Robot	h.11″	Plastic head sometimes damaged.	5
97E.	Chief Smoky	h.11″		5
97F.	Chief Robot Man	h.11″	Many color variations.	5
98A.				4
98B.				4
98C.	Zoomer	h.8″	Many color variations.	4
98D.	Radar Robot	h.9″		5
98E.	Musical Drumming Robot	h.8″		5
99A.	Wheelbarrow Robot	h.12″	Wheelbarrow sometimes missing.	4
99B.	Forklift Robot	h.12″	The box he carries is often missing.	5
99C.	Original Lost in Space Robot	h.12″	Bottom plate that holds batteries is sometimes broken. Head is usually split.	3
99D.	Lost in Space Robot	h.10″		2
100A.	Gigantor	h.8½″		3
100B.	Robot Control	h.7″		4
100C.	Golden Roto Robot	h.8½″	Legs sometimes cracked where they are attached to the body.	2
100D.	Talking Robot	h.10″	Talk is sometimes garbled.	4
100E.	Mike Robot	h.12″	Microphone often doesn't work.	4
100F.	Piston Head Robot	h.9″		3
101A.	Moonlight Man	h.12″	One of a large series of Japanese super heros.	3
101B.	Mat Astronaut	h.12″		3
101C.	Millerman	h.13″		3
101D.	Astronaut	h.14″	Dome sometimes cracked or missing.	4
101E.	Gigantor	h.13″		5
102A.	Smoking Spaceman	h.12″	Smoke sometimes not working.	5
102B.	Wheel - A - Gear Robot	h.16″	Rubberband in chest usually needs replacing.	5
not shown	Blink - A - Gear Robot		Variation of 102B	4
102C.	Rosko Astronaut	h.12½″	The dome is sometimes cracked and the buzzer doesn't always work.	5
103A.				
103B.	Mr. Mercury	h.12½″	The foam handpads are often worn, and an easily broken die cast gear controls bending.	5
103C.	Space Explorer	h.12″	Extremely difficult to repair. Several variations.	5
103D	Mr. Atomic	h.9″	Dome is sometimes cracked. Also a blue variation.	6
104A.	Robotank Z	h.10″	Plastic pinion gear.	4
not shown	Talking Robotank Z	h.10″	Variation of 104A, speaks Japanese.	4
not shown	Robotank R-I	h.10″	Earlier version of 104A.	4
104B.	Space Commander	h.10″		3
104C.	Thunder Robot	h.12″	Antenna is sometimes missing	5
104D.	Dino	h.12″	Head sometimes sticks in the open position.	4
105A.				5
105B.	Directional Robot	h.10½″		5
105C.	Radar Robot	h.11″		5
105D.	Robot	h.9″		5
105E.	Robot 8	h.12″	Pinion gear sometimes needs replacing.	5
106A.	Mini Robotank	h.4½″	Has a plastic pinion gear.	3
106B.	Walking Robot	h.6″	The dome is very fragile. Also an undomed variation.	4
106C.	Mini Robotank TR2	h.4½″	Has a plastic pinion gear.	3
106D.	Powder Robot	h.7½″		5
106E.	Robot	h.6″		5
106F.	Mr. Robot Mechanical Brain	h.8″		4
107A.	Engine Robot	h.8½″	Several variations.	3

h.=height   l.=length

No.	NAME	SIZE	COMMENTS	DESIRABILITY
107B.	Robot	h.9″	Also a silver version.	4
107C.	Space Scout	h.8½″	Also a silver variation.	4
not shown	Mr. Xerox	h.8½″	Robot version of 107C.	4
107D.	Gear Robot	h.11″	The plastic front is sometimes cracked.	4
107E.	Mr. Patrol	h.11″		4
not shown	Robot version of Mr. Patrol	h.11″	Similar to 107E.	5
107F.	Turn Signal Robot	h.11″	Plastic front sometimes cracks.	4
108A.	Robot Commando	h.20″	Has many parts which may be missing.	2
108B.	Pepo	h.30″		4
109A.	Hysterical Harry	h.13″		3
109B.	Giant Robot	h.14″		3
109C.	Mr. Lem	h.13″		2
109D.	Gear Robot	h.12½″		2
109E.	Krome Dome	h.11″		3
109F.	Lunar Spaceman	h.11½″		2
110A.	Dalek	h.6″	American batteries are slightly too large for the battery box. Several variations.	3
110B.	Tiny Robot	h.4″		3
110C.	Talking Dalek	h.6″	From *Dr. Who* T.V. show.	2
not shown	Talking K-9 (Robot Dog.)		Also from *Dr. Who.*	2
110D.	Explo	h.7½″		2
110E.	Mr. Brain	l.10″		3
110F.	Jupiter Robot	h.6″		3
111A.	Missile Robot	h.9″	One of a large series of 70's Robots.	1
111B.	Mr. Monster	h.11″		1
111C.	Mr. Mercury	h.10″	One of a series of 70's Robots.	1
111D.	Space Explorer	h.12″	Many different versions.	2
111E.	Attacking Martian	h.10″	One of a very large series of 60's & 70's Robots.	2
111F.	Swivel - O - Matic Astronaut	h.12″	Many variations.	2
112A.	City Bus	l.14″		2
112B.	School Bus	l.13″		3
112C.	Sound Bus	l.15″		2
112D.	Sight Seeing Bus	l.9″		4
113A.	Motorcycle	l.11½″	Very complex mechanism.	5
113B.	Police Motorcycle	l.11½″	Very complex mechanism.	5
113C.	Mystery Jet Plane	l.10½″		4
113D.	Highway Patrol Car	l.15½″		4
114A.	Television Truck	l.11″		4
114B.	NBC Truck	l.8″		4
114C.	Railroad Handcar	l.10″		4
114D.	Forklift Truck	l.10″		3
115A.	Merry Go Round Truck	l.10″		4
115B.	All Trains (various sizes)		Most are very difficult to sell. Many variations.	1-2
115C.				
115D.				
115E.	All Tractors and Bulldozers (various sizes)		Many variations	1-3
116A.	All Fire Engines (various sizes)		Many variations.	1-4
116B.	Coke Truck	l.11″		4
116C.	Jeep	l.10″		2
116D.	Combat Tank	l.9″		2
117A.	Ocean Liner	l.20″		5
117B.	Aircraft Carrier	l. 20″	Many small parts sometimes missing.	5
117C.	All Speedboats (various sizes)		Many variations.	1-3
117D.	Nautilus Sub	l.14″		4
117E.	Captain Kidd Pirate Ship	l.13″		3
118A.	Mars Rocket	l.13″		4
118B.	Space Captain	l.12″		4
118C.	Cape Canaveral Truck	l.8″	Space version of NBC truck.	4

No.	NAME	SIZE	COMMENTS	DESIRABILITY
118D.	Space Survey Saucer	l.8″		4
118E.	Space Patrol Tank	l.10″		4
119A.	Piston Tractor	l.9″	Battery cases often corroded.	4
119B.	Radar Tractor	l.9″		4
119C.	Robot Tractor	l.9″		4
119D.	Space Robot Car	l.11″	Often missing parts.	5
119E.	Robot Bulldozer	l.8″		4
119F.	Robot Car X-9	l.10″	Dome sometimes cracked.	5
120A.	1960's Plymouth TV Wagon	l.12″		4
120B.	1950's Plymouth	l.11½″		4
121A.	1950's Cadillac	l.12″		6
121B.	1950's Cadillac Convertible	l.12″		5
121C.	1960's Cadillac	l.12″		4
122.	1950's Buick	l.7½″	Friction motors - Battery operated lights only.	5
123A.	1950's Thunderbird	l.11″		5
123B.	1950's Thunderbird Convertible	l.11″		6
123C.	1950's Thunderbird	l.12″		4
124A.	1960's Corvette	l.11″		5
124B.	1960's Corvette	l.10″		3
124C.	1960's Corvette	l.10″		3
125A.	1960's Mustang	l.12″		4
125B.	1960's Mustang	l.11″		4
125C.	1960's Mustang	l.10″	Racing decals detract from value.	2
126A.	1950's Benz	l.10½″		5
126B.	(See box section)			
126C.	1950's Benz Racer	l.10″		4
127A.	1960's 220 S Benz	l.11½″		5
127B.	1960's Benz	l.13″		4
127C.	1960's Benz Taxi	l.10″		4
128A.	1960's Volkswagon	l.9½″		4
128B.	1960's Bolkswagon	l.13″		4
128C.	1960's Volkswagon Convertible	l.9½″		4
128D.	1960's Volkswagon Convertible	l.13″		5
129A.	1960's Volkswagon Convertible	l.8″	Plastic pinion gear.	3
129B.	1960's Volkswagon	l.8″	Plastic pinion gear.	2
129C.	1960's Volkswagon Microbus	l.10″		4
129D.	1960's Volkswagon Pick-Up	l.8″		3
130A.	1960's Porsche	l.10″		4
130B.	1960's Porsche	l.8½″		2
130C.	1960's Jaguar	l.10″		4
131A.	1960's Rolls Royce	l.12″		5
131B.	1960's Ferrari	l.11″	Plastic pinion gear.	4
131C.	1960's Citroen	l.12″		5
132A.	1950's Opel	l.11″		5
132B.	1950's Lincoln	l.12″		4
132C.	1950's Mercury	l.9″		4
133A.	1960's Camero	l.10″		2
133B.	1960's Pontiac Firebird	l.10″		3
133C.	1960's Cougar	l.10″		2
134A.	1960's Ford	l.12″	Possibly late 1950's.	4
134B.	1960's Ford GT	l.12″		3
134C.	1960's Toronado	l.10½″		3
135A.	1960's Corvair	l.12″		4
135B.	1960's Sea Hawk	l.13″		3
135C.	1960's Ford Gyron	l.10½″	Also a red and black remote control version.	4
137A.	Great Garloo	h.24″	Usually missing medallion.	4

h.=height   l.=length

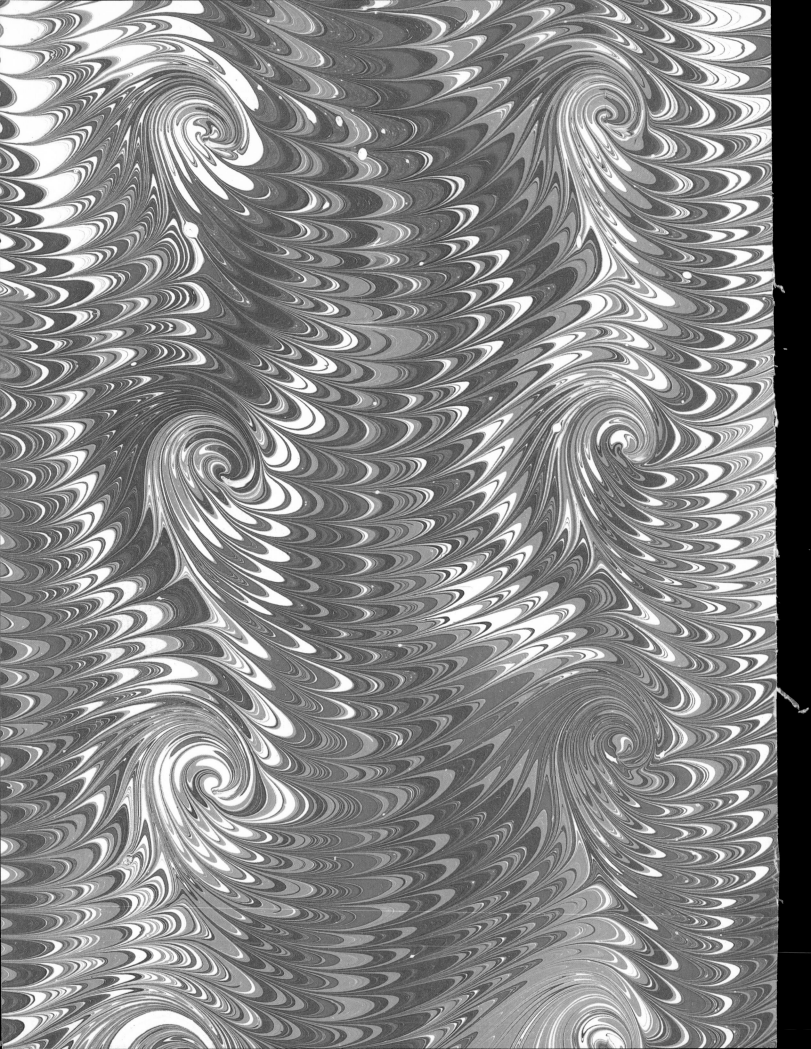